Life Does Get Better
Peace Within is Found Again

By:
Sara Khan

Printing History: First Edition, First Printing, March 2016.

ISBN-13: 978-1530513796

ISBN-10: 1530513790

Dedications

I would like to dedicate my book to the following people:

My darling husband who has stood with me through all my hard times - believe me there have been many. To my two beautiful children who I will always protect as you are my responsibility, my world and I will never take my eyes off you.

My sister-in- laws, who are like my blood sisters and who have stood by me through all my troubles.

Jennifer Don, who inspired me to write down my feelings into poems and who has guided me onto the path that I am on today, and to Jayne Colligan and Asif Choudary for helping me set up my various websites, which thousands have looked at and will continue to do so.

Riff Haworth, who has helped me put my book together and supported me as a friend, and to Fleur Everall, for reading my book and giving me the extra support I needed by being there.

To all my friends around the world, who have listened to me over the years and being there for me?

My brothers- I will always love you, and I am sorry that you had to experience this pain. Things DO get better and in time and you will get stronger.

To the Spirit World who have been with me throughout my life, and are continuing with me on my journey ahead - thank you for being there for me.

This is my gift to all the victims out there; believe me it can be done - I am living proof of that. You will know when the time is right to begin your journey. My life DID get better and I have found my inner peace within.

This is my story. My hope is that in some way, it helps others find their own inner peace.

Contents

Introduction

 was browsing the net and came across a website, where I began to write how happy I was, when someone asked me how I had gotten to that stage. As I started to answer their question, I had thought: "I could explain this in a book." I felt a spirit presence as this thought was going through my mind. I often get visits from spirits, and lately, these experiences had been getting stronger each day.

I believe I was led by the spirit world and by my gut instinct to write this book, to explain how I found my inner peace, which is so powerful: strong and yet so calming.

There was a stage in my life when I gave up, and lost sight of the person I was, but I have found myself again. I was groomed and sexually abused as a child, until my teens; I believe that what happened to me was maybe written in my destiny and is what fate had in store for me. I had to go through that terrible time in my life to get to where I am now. I will never forget what happened to me, but with time and with determination I have healed. It is in my past --and that is where it belongs.

Bad things happened to me, but I have survived to tell my story, Take it from me, I am a survivor--after all, I am still here. There are times in my life I could have died, or I could have ended with a life in the gutter, but that was not meant to be. Fate had destined for me to survive and to tell my story, so I could help other victims become survivors, too.

I want to say to anyone reading this who feels that they are a victim: You are ultimately in control of your life, and you do not need to stay a victim forever. You will know when it is the right time to fight, and you will get stronger with each step you take. Always look forward, not back, and you will be rewarded. Things do not always stay the same.

***

I am of Asian heritage, in my forties, and known by the name of Sara; I was born and brought up in a large, traditional Hindu family. I have one sister, three brothers, grandparents and lots of cousins, aunts and uncles. Then there was the extended family, where everyone knew each other's business, who brought over traditional values from the Punjab and reinforced them onto us. They thought they were doing the right thing, forgetting the fact that we were British and lived in a Western world. We were brought up in an Indian household, but sent to an English school, whilst still adoring Asian values. I do believe, though, that these opposing influences could have worked, if they had been enforced correctly.

My family was well known in the community and highly respected. We were made to believe everything was well, but, as is the case in every community, (no matter how 'closely knit') no-one ever really knows what happens behind closed doors. I soon realised, as I was growing up, that it was very important to give a good impression to the outside world, in order to keep the 'family honour' intact.

If people do find out the truth about what really does go on, that family is scarred for life. That is why what happens behind closed doors stays inside those four walls. People put on a smile and an innocent face, and life carries on regardless. People go about their business as normal, visiting each other and pretending that they love each other. In reality, these are mere formalities that have to be carried out in a convincing way.

Only a handful of people in such communities escape the

traditional family values which are brought back from their native country. I am one of the people from such a community who broke family tradition by leaving home and setting up on my own.

I am married to a Muslim man who is hard-working and someone I look up to. I have two lovely boys whom I adore, and a network of friends, along with a handful of family members, whom I love dearly. I work for a big organisation and love my job. I have met many lovely people, some of whom, in time, have become good friends. I have become a happy person who is content with her life; I feel I have everything that I could ever want.

But things have not always been like this .I have struggled with life, shed tears, cried out to family, and begged for help, for forty years. Hurting inside and in pain, I have taken overdoses, self-harmed, and drunk vast amounts of alcohol to try to block the pain; I have sat in front of my mother with a bottle of wine hoping she would see my pain and get me some help. I just wanted to be at peace and clear of the hurt, the sadness, and the memories that haunted me. I couldn't see a way out.

Despite this, I tried hard to carry on doing my best in everything I did. Being well-practised at putting on a front, I gave the impression of being a strong, positive woman. Trying to be positive and to face whatever challenges life threw at me, made me feel in control. I was in charge of my body and soul, not my abusers.

It's not easy to forget though, what my abusers and my family put me through. I have come to terms with it now, but I need to share my story, to encourage others, to let them know that it is worth the wait in the end- that there is light at the end of the tunnel.

I was only a daughter by birth (as I was reminded again and again). I was made to feel I was entirely to blame for what happened to me; I became an outcast to my entire family, and I wasn't allowed to attend family functions, apart from a selected few. I remember watching my siblings get ready to go to family weddings, parties, and functions organised by others. No one really asked why I wasn't going; I just had to make excuses, and help my family keep the' family honour'.

I used to beg my mom to let me tell my brothers and my sister. Her excuse for the secrecy was always the same: "No one will give their hand in marriage to your siblings if people find out." So I kept my secret in order to protect my siblings, and suffered in silence. I truly thought I was helping the family by keeping it to myself, and in my own heart, I craved their acceptance. I wanted so much to belong in their world, and to be wanted by them, too.

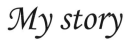

My story

My nightmare began at the age of three.

It was at this age that I first suffered sexual abuse at the hands of my father's brother; my uncle. At this age I also witnessed a rape that happened in front of my sister, my brother, and me.

It began while we were living at my grandmother's house. I was just a little girl who craved my family's love and trust; I did not understand what was happening. I suffered in silence, so much wanting to speak to someone, but becoming frozen with fear at the mere thought of actually doing it.

Although I wasn't aware at the time, I discovered when I grew up that all the elders in the family knew about the abuse that I had suffered with the first uncle, whilst it was happening. I found out that my mom had told my dad and his reply was merely that "all men do this- it's normal behaviour."

The abuse stopped when I was 8 years old, because of plans made to go abroad to visit family in India for six weeks. My nightmare resumed soon after we got there, when another uncle (my mom's brother) began to abuse me too.

I was only eight, and this would happen when we would visit him at his house. I was so confused and lost in a world of my own. Was this normal behaviour? Did all girls go through this? That question would go round and round in my head. When we left India to go home, I was ok for a while. I felt safe back at my parents' house, which I saw as my comfort zone. 'No one can touch me now', I told myself (even though my first abuser was living next door). I felt safe, my ordeal was over, and I could be a little girl again.

Total shock hit me two years later when I heard that the same uncle that had abused me in India was coming to England to get married, and he was going to live with us. When he arrived, I was ten, and I had blanked out from my mind what had happened in India. The sexual abuse started again, and continued into my teens.

Why didn't I speak up? I ask myself as I write this, and can hear you asking too. Who to? Who would listen to me? Would anything change? I had already told the adults in my life, when it first started happening, but they had allowed it to continue by doing nothing to stop it.

I hated my life so much that I started to self-harm. I remember my auntie finding me doing this. She did not question me, and I think this was because she did not want to hear the answer.

One day, I was in my dad's shed in the back garden. I was crying so much, I was so upset, but no one was around. Then I saw a bottle of paraffin and I drank it, thinking that this could be my way out. I was found and spent some time in hospital, but again, no questions were asked.

I just wanted to end my life and be free of the pain that I was suffering. Why did they choose me and not my sister? Was it the fact that I was pretty with a nice pale face, whereas my sister was darker in colour and skinny? I wished so much that I was ugly; maybe then they wouldn't have looked at me, I told myself. But it was me they chose, and me they tried to destroy.

I truly believed throughout my childhood that I didn't mean anything to anyone and that the reason for this could be that maybe I was adopted. I was so lost and confused, feeling different; feeling alienated, believing that I didn't belong in this family.

Even after I had taken numerous overdoses, still no one asked me why. I used to take my mom's medicine, hoping that it was dangerous and that it would end my suffering. I remember, in my pain, feeling glad that it was me who had this pain though, and not my sister, as if, in going through it myself, I was protecting her.

Looking back at my years in primary school, I felt different. I was taller than the other children were, with long black hair tied up in two ponytails. I remember sitting on the floor with the other children, not interacting and feeling confused.

Even at this early stage of my childhood, I felt that I didn't fit in. I chose not to talk to anyone, preferring to keep to myself. I managed to make a couple of friends, who also seemed lost. Maybe we all fitted in nicely. I remember one occasion, when I was sat at a desk, and the teacher put his hand on my knee. This made me feel uncomfortable. Looking back, I can see that he most probably did it unintentionally. He wasn't aware of what I was going through.

Then there were the times I couldn't put my hand up to ask questions, because I was always holding myself back. My little voice would stay at the back of my throat. No matter what I did, nothing came out; it was as if I had lost my voice.

I didn't really enjoy school activities, and would make excuses to get myself out of them. I remember a dancing rehearsal with some boys, which I managed to get out of.

At the age of ten, I started my periods, and I felt different, again, as I believed I was the only girl who had. It became a good excuse to get out of activities I had already felt uncomfortable about.

I have strong memories of one particular day at primary school when the teacher asked me to tidy the bookshelf up. I didn't really know then, but looking back, I realise I had spirit with me, even then. The strong smell that I get now was with me. I remember at the time, feeling as if someone was with me, but couldn't really put it down to anything. (As I write this, I have spirit with me; that lovely, sweet smell). I realise now that spirit has been with me, comforting me and making me feel safe, from an early age, but I didn't realise what it was until later on in life.

I remember a time when my brother and sister were playing and cuddling each other. They would have been five and six and I was seven. I used to look at them, and think to myself '" that doesn't seem right, why isn't my mom stopping them?" Looking back, I recognise that this is normal behaviour for children, and is something they should all have the right to do without embarrassment or shame. But I was not a normal child; I was confused, and lived in my own little world. At the same time, I felt left out and I wanted to join in, but I didn't like to be touched. So I chose to stay in my little world where I felt safe – it wasn't worth the risk to venture away from it.

Later memories include travelling to London as a teenager, with my family, to visit other family members. My mom's brother was travelling with us and everyone seemed to be showing him so much respect. His wife, my mum and my younger siblings were all in the same car. At one point, my auntie said she was going to have a nap and asked me if I could talk to my uncle to keep him busy whilst he was driving. I didn't say anything to him, feeling awkward in his presence. My voice wouldn't come out. All I could feel was his presence and this made me so uncomfortable. When we arrived at our destination, I tried to stay away from him as best as I could. I thought to myself, "I am safe here, lots of people around" - all I had to do was stay well clear. My little head was running overtime again, trying to find ways I could keep my distance.

One night, I was asleep next to his wife in someone else's house, with my mom in the same room. The next thing I remember being woken up by my uncle making a pass at me. I couldn't believe it - in someone else's house and his wife next to me. I pushed him away and all I could smell was fumes of whisky. I stayed awake all night, terrified. That night, I held my tears in, as I didn't want anyone to hear me.

I don't ever remember my mum hugging me. I always felt distant from her .She was never at home, either working or out visiting relatives. They spent a lot of time visiting, which meant we were often left on our own, or with other members of family. I suppose she felt it was safe to do so, even knowing what had happened to me. But I didn't feel safe.

At the age of fourteen and at senior school, I unintentionally disclosed the abuse I was suffering to a family member whilst describing an event connected to it, although I did not actually say that I was being abused. This person told my mom and the next thing I remember was my mom beating me up as punishment for my cry for help. I didn't understand what I had said was wrong, so I couldn't see why I was being punished. As usual, I tried to continue with life as best as I could.

At sixteen, I had a boyfriend and everything seemed to be going okay. I liked him, and I liked the feeling of being wanted. Having someone to listen to me and to cuddle up to was nice. I felt for the first time that I actually had a purpose in life. I had strong feelings for this boy, and I felt for the first time in my life valued for who I was.

We had been seeing each other for a few weeks when his sister came to see me to tell me that her brother could not go out with me any more. Devastated and hurt, I asked why. "Your uncle beat him up," was her reply. I just looked at her. What could I say? I felt broken and in pieces. I carried on as usual, trying to get on with life.

I was engaged at seventeen, to a man my family had chosen for me. I thought this would be a way out, and although I didn't have any feelings for him, I agreed to marry him. I saw this as my escape route from the hell I was in.

I married him abroad and I knew he genuinely liked me, but I still felt nothing for him. As soon as I came back to the UK, I realised I had made a mistake and wanted so much to get out of this situation. I did not want to proceed with the formality of getting married again in the UK. I plucked up the courage to tell my family that I could not go through with the wedding. Their response was unsurprisingly not favourable, as all they appeared to be bothered about was the family honour.' Your brothers and sister are not married yet, no one will look at us', they told me. They would spend hours and hours trying to get me change my mind.

In the end, I had to tell them the real reason why I couldn't get married. I told my mom and my auntie that my dad's brother had sexually abused me from the age of three.

My auntie was educated, whereas my mom wasn't, so I think I expected more from her than I did from mom. I had told them something very serious, expecting someone to do something to stop it. I needed help, sympathy, someone to hold me and tell me it was all going to be alright, but none was forthcoming.

Again, it was just brushed under the carpet. If only someone had come back to me, maybe I would have revealed everything, and might have even spoken about the abuse from my other uncle, too. Looking back, I don't think I was ready to tell them at that time, but I wonder if I could have been saved from further years of abuse. I didn't realise then, as I do now, that they were more concerned about protecting 'family honour.'

My mom's brother continued to abuse me. He was fifty years old and I was seventeen. His wife must have told him about the abuse from my other uncle, which I had previously told her about. I wasn't really sure if she had mentioned it to him or not, all I know is that he started to be supportive, He would sit and listen to me pouring my heart out and crying. I was so messed up with everything that was happening in my life. Despite my revelations about being abused, I was still pressured to go ahead with the marriage. I just could not understand this, and the resulting turmoil led to another overdose, as I could not take any more of this pain. I was rushed to hospital, had my stomach pumped, and was left again to suffer in silence.

My second uncle's wife and my mom found out about the sexual abuse a few years later, and it stopped. They must have said something to him but no one appeared concerned about my well-being, as no-one asked how I was. I was free of the sexual abuse, but was left with the emotional scars. I was not aware that I could get help - it hadn't crossed my mind that I was a victim. I was made to believe I was the one to blame, and, in my head, I believed this to be true.

My uncle and his wife visited Mom regularly. I would just blank them out. I was hurting inside, and yet I still had to put up with him being around, being near me. The thought of getting any help never occurred to me, as I truly believed I was at fault. So again, I continued with my life, carrying the pain inside me.

One day, my second uncle and cousin came to my workplace, looking for me. I was not at work that day; I had not gone in, and they were determined to find me and find out what I had been doing. They had waited for me to get home, and were parked up in their car very close by when I got back. As I was approaching my house, they shouted for me and asked me to get in the car. They went mad at me, demanding to know where I had been, as I had not been at work. I was not allowed to have any life outside of work and family. This made me feel ignored, ostracised and suffocated--all at the same time.

They said they were going to tell my mom what I had been doing. My cousin left to go in the house and I exploded at my uncle, telling him that after what he did to me, he had no right to tell me what to do. I said I was going to tell everyone he had abused me over the years. He started crying, begging me not to say anything, but I didn't care, I'd just about had enough of this pain and hurt.

I hesitated about telling the family straight away, as I couldn't bring myself to do it. I went to work, and told a few people there instead. This was the first time I had spoken to an outsider about my experience. I didn't want to leave work that day, as I was scared to go home, but I knew today was the day I must tell them. People at work encouraged me to go home and face them, and I did.

As I was telling my cousin's wife in my bedroom, my mom was sitting at the edge of the bed. Mom already knew what had happened, but I don't think she knew how badly and to what extent I had been traumatized. I told my cousin's wife about my uncles sexually abusing me. Both she and my mom left the room and they didn't return. Yet again, I was left with this heavy burden on my shoulders to bear alone – it seemed that none of my family was prepared to offer help and support, or to come up with the solutions I desperately needed. I carried on suffering in silence and began to blame myself again.

A few weeks later, my cousin took me to live with him and his family in London. He tried to help me in the way he thought was best. I tried to be positive, looking upon it as an opportunity for a new beginning as I was away from my abusers at last.

On the outside, I was making progress; I got myself a job and I bought my own car. Inside, though, I was still hurting so much. I wanted to lash out and cry, but who was I to cry to? No-one was there for me, no-one wanted to listen. I did call my younger brother, who was sixteen at the time. I cannot remember what I said to him, but was later told that I had been in tears. I was on the phone for two hours, crying my eyes out and telling him what had happened. He was only young, what could he have done? My cousin told me later that he had tried to speak to my uncle, but he had refused to come to the phone.

Then my cousin started to introduce me to guys whom he thought I might marry. I remember at least one guy who was pleasant enough, but I just wasn't ready for marriage. When I told my cousin this, he started shouting at me, saying there was something wrong with me. I was very upset but tried not to show it. I went upstairs, put all my stuff into a black bag, and hid it. I intended to go to work as normal the next morning, but not to return to my cousin's.

I was working as a nanny at the time, looking after a baby and a toddler. What I did next seems crazy when I think about it now, but I just wanted to escape. I booked a ticket to go to America that evening. Looking back, it seems a stupid thing to do; but the fact that I had no connections there meant that no-one would know me or my past. It was my chance to make a clean break and a new start. The only person I remotely knew there was a man I had met in my old job. I had his address and that was it - he was my only means of contact there. This was an unplanned, spur-of-the-moment decision. Looking back on it now, I can see that this was a means of escaping from my life of misery and rejection.

I went to the airport, and waited for my plane to arrive. I tried to sell my car but no one was interested, so I just left it in the car park and went to sit in the airport. I had a good few hours to wait before I could board the plane and sat waiting and thinking. I was all alone again. I started to feel panicky and scared, so I called a friend I had met through a previous job. She came to meet me at the airport and took me to her house. I didn't know what I was going to do, but I felt I had finally escaped from my family. Despite this and everything I had been through, I knew deep down that I still loved them dearly.

My Spiritual Journey Begins

managed to find rented accommodations in London, but soon felt alone and isolated again. I found out my family was looking for me, and it was only a matter of time before they did find me. When they did find me, I told them I wasn't going back home and they accepted that. I continued living on my own and got myself a job, but I was still not at peace. I would cry at night until my pillow was drenched. I knew I was heading for a nervous breakdown.

One night, I was so upset I didn't want to go to sleep. I made myself stay awake and something happened. I didn't know at the time but I started to have an out-of- body experience. (This is when your soul comes out of your body).

While I was out of my body, I saw another spirit floating in my room. I heard a 'hello' from this spirit, which frightened me so much that I 'jumped back' into my body again. This was the start of my out-of-body experiences, a phenomenon that was to last for twenty years.

In time, I learned a bit more about what was happening. I was aware of what was going on, but at that time, I didn't know how to stop it. I could see myself out of my body and I would try to switch the light on--but nothing would happen. I tried to move my body or try to wake up, but I could not. This was a very frightening time for me. After twenty years. I remember asking them; 'please leave me alone' and somehow, it worked. I didn't have the experiences again until later, although during this break, I still felt a spirit presence around me at all times.

I would call my mom at regular intervals and cry to her for help, begging for her to do something, to tell my brothers and my sister what happened to me. She always refused to do this, telling me that the family honour was more important than anything. As well as mom, everyone else too chose to be blind to my efforts to alert them and my obvious signs of personal breakdown.

The elders in the family all knew, as I had gradually told every one of them. In doing so, I suffered the consequences by being completely cut off by yet another family member. I found it hard to understand why this was happening over and over again; why the only action taken was to ostracise me even more.

I kept in contact with my family, but I never went back home. The family told relatives I was living with my cousin. No one really knew the truth: that I had chosen to live by myself. I kept their family honour, something which was more important to them than I was.

I would attend family functions and be the daughter they wanted. Inside, I was in pain. I watched my abusers in their 'uncle' roles, well- respected in the family circle, standing with their wives, who were well aware of what they had done to me. I wished I could know what was going through their heads as I watched them carrying out their wifely duties. Family honour always came first in our family, not their women's, their daughter's feelings. For the following twenty years I continued coming up and down to attend family functions, putting on a brave face in my attempt to hide the truth about my feelings.

My sister got married for the second time, and she again had a big wedding. I know I should not be jealous. It was not written in my destiny to have such a wedding myself. I dutifully carried out my role of elder daughter to the best of my ability. I held my head up high and did not even glance at my abusers. I put on a smile and danced happily. I had to show them that they had no control over me, that it was me who was in control, not them, and this was my life, not theirs. They could not see the tears that I was holding back, and I didn't want them to. I could not avoid being in their presence, though, trying not to think what might be going through their head.

A few days after my sister's wedding, I was talking with my cousin and could not believe what she was telling me. She said that my uncle (on my mom's side) had been touching her in a way that she knew was not right. I did not want to believe that this was happening again. I had already told my family about what this uncle had done to me. Why were they letting it happen again? My cousin did not know as she was telling me, about the abuse I suffered at the hands of that same uncle. I decided to tell her and my aunties what had happened to me. Again, it was left at that, no-one said to me 'let's get you some help'. This response was typical, and as always, made me feel that I was the one at fault.

Because of this, I never even tried myself to get help. I was left to suffer again in silence. Our parents chose to do nothing about what our uncle did to us, their daughters. They were more concerned about their daughters' honour being at stake and the difficulty they would have getting us married if the truth were to come out.

Then, at my cousin's wedding, I saw a guy; there was something about him that I liked. I asked my cousin to find out if he would go out with me. My cousin turned around and told me that he was an educated man, and therefore "he won't go out with you." I then asked my mom and grandmother if I could marry this guy. They said no, as he was from a different caste from me. I left it at that and I returned to London.

That is where I met my husband. I was working as a traffic warden and he must have seen me. He came over to me and asked me out. I was not interested at first, but something made me say yes to him. We started dating. I went back to mum's, where my cousin asked me if I was still interested in his friend. I was annoyed at my cousin and I told him it was too late. The guy I had seen at the wedding wasn't meant for me; it wasn't written in my destiny. I chose a different path.

I continued my relationship with the guy who is now my

husband. When I introduced him to my family, they were not happy that I had chosen a Muslim. I found this hard to swallow. Did they not want me to be happy?

We decided to get married a few years later. I had to beg my mom to come to my wedding. I wanted it to be a big occasion with all my family there but I was told I couldn't, as if it was a big wedding, my uncles would have to be there. I married my husband surrounded by friends and my sister- in- laws. It was a small wedding, and deep down, I missed my family being there.

Whilst I was working as a traffic warden, a member of the public punched me. This brought my past to the surface, and I started to have out-of-body experiences again. I was off work for three months, as I was so traumatised. I saw a doctor about my nightmares, and I told her about my past. She recommended that I had some counselling and to report my abusers to the police but I did not feel strong enough. I had to protect my family honour. So I just carried on with my life as best as I could. My husband and I would go and visit my family two to three times a year. That was enough for me, as one of my abusers was living next door to my mom's and the other just down the road, so they were always in and out of her house. I would always clam up when I saw them.

My husband knew about my past, as I had told him when I first met him. I had to really. He knew something was badly wrong as I was always crying and taking too much medication. I was surprised he did not leave me, as I was such a mess. I know he loves me, as he has always been there for me. He would hold my hand whenever we saw my abusers. I had told him not to do anything, as I had to keep the family honour. It was very hard for him--but he did it for me.

My Mom was holding Rahki—a tradition where siblings show each other their love--at her house on one occasion. Mom was tying a piece of thread onto her brother, to represent love. I was sitting in the front room, holding my husband's hand as tight as I could. It hurt me a lot, seeing my mother show love to my uncle, knowing what he had done to me. Mom tried to explain that she had to carry on being with my uncles, because they had to keep the family honour intact. She kept in touch with my abusers and went to visit them regularly.

I had my first baby at the age of thirty-seven. Spirits often visited me in the early hours of awakening .One morning I was lying in bed and I heard music in my ears. This was the spirit world giving me one of their messages. One song I remember from the time of my pregnancy was "It's going to be ok." I had a hospital appointment one morning, and spirits were talking to me whilst I was there, which scared me at the time as I wasn't aware of what was happening.

When my baby boy was born, my emotional pain eased slightly, as I had my baby to look after now. I brought my baby home and thought how empty the house seemed: there was just my husband, baby and me--no relatives. I spent the first day by myself with the baby. My mom came the following week to help me, which was nice, but we didn't really have much to say to each other. She returned home after a short while, and I felt all alone. I stopped crying as much, but my nightmares did not go away.

I would visit Mom only every now and again with my baby; honestly, I was scared to face my abusers. I also noticed that some extended family members did not appear to accept my child. I told myself it wasn't important; nonetheless, it did affect me. My family never really came to visit me. I had a big family, some of whom I still felt close to, but I very rarely saw any of them. When I did see them, they showed me love and I truly believed that they loved my children and me. That wasn't the case, as I later found out, when I was sorting out my past. It was all false love, to keep me sweet and keep their family honour intact.

My Life was to Change Forever

 t was at my brother's wedding that my life started to change. The wedding was to start on Saturday and my granddad died on Monday. This was a very emotional time for me, as my Granddad had not spoken to me in twenty years. I saw this as due to the fact that I married a Muslim, and fact that his son abused me; he knew what had happened to me from an early age. He was also aware about the abuse from the second uncle--but to him, my marrying a Muslim was worse than any of that.

I had tried to speak to granddad during the years that I visited Mom. I also introduced my husband to him, but Granddad soon dismissed him, ordering him out of the house. Granddad—or Baba, as I sometimes called him--lived next door to my family home with my uncle and his family. I remember once asking my cousin if he could take a message to my granddad: 'When Baba (Granddad) dies, I will not be coming to his funeral.' I would not have gone either, had it not been that he died when I was at Mom's. I heard the cries of everyone in the early hours of the morning.

I had said I was not going to come to his funeral, but it was as if he had purposefully waited until I was there so that I could not avoid it. In the past, I had tried to make amends with him but recently and much to my regret, I had given up trying, as he had on so many previous occasions refused to speak to me.

I hated him for leaving me out and doing so much for my sister and her family. I had everything I ever wanted in my husband and baby, but I still felt left out. When she had her children, she was showered with gifts and money. She got money and gifts when she got married for the second time too. I saw this as being very unfair, especially as she has been married twice.

In contrast, I got nothing from Granddad, and so I did feel jealous and left out. It wasn't the money side of things that bothered me - I just wanted his love and acceptance. I wanted to belong in his world, and to hear him say he loved me. But he just seemed to have cut me out of his life.

The funeral was on a Friday, and I went to see his body. He was lying in the coffin looking peaceful. Moreover, he must have been laughing at me standing there over him. He was my granddad, and I know deep down he loved me. This was confirmed to me a few years previously, when in the early morning I had one of my experiences in which I heard his voice. He was calling my brother's name aloud. Spirits have always spoken to me in the early hours of awakening. I thought then he might have passed away, but I believe it was his consciousness speaking out loud. I had been recently telling my brother that granddad never spoke to me for twenty years and he had replied by saying he had no idea and it wasn't the time for this conversation. As usual, it wasn't my time and again, I had to keep my feelings locked in.

The wedding started on Saturday and it was such an emotional time. Granddad's passing had come unexpectedly and we were all sad. However, we had to show our support to our brother as it was his special day. My brother married a Japanese girl, which was hard for me to take in, because of the negative response I had got from my family when I introduced my Muslim husband to them. It took them years to accept him.

I have nothing against my brother and his wife but I do feel angry about it deep down. Why didn't my family accept my husband and me in the same way? I would have loved a big wedding with all my family there, but in reality I had to beg my family to attend my wedding and my mom only came at the last minute. Why was it different for me? I know why, deep down, the reason they could not have a big wedding for me; they would have had to invite my abusers. This, in hindsight, proves to me that they cared more for the family honour and keeping things running smoothly than my happiness and well-being.

A week before the wedding, I had phoned my mom and again cried my eyes out. I asked her 'please can I tell my brothers, as I cannot take this pain anymore?' Mom said 'no' and began emotionally blackmailing me again. I know deep down that it wasn't the right time, but I felt I couldn't go through with facing my abusers again. Therefore, to keep the family honour, I carried on with my family duties. I was the daughter that they wanted me to be; one to be proud of.

For twenty years, I went along doing my duties as a daughter, In front of the extended family and knowing that all the elders were aware of the abuse. Not one of them asked me how I was feeling. They merely kept up the pretence of caring for me. While the rest of the family were included in the family gatherings, I was left out and it hurt.

When I started trying to sort out my past out at forty years old, I found out Mom had told everyone in the family that if my uncles were attending the function, I wasn't to be invited. She thought she was protecting me by doing this. This led to me being left out and my uncles not being affected in any way: things just carried on as normal for them. No wonder I thought I was to blame. Mom did apologise to me much later for doing this; she thought she was doing the right thing.

The wedding was just great. I would say it was one of the best weddings I had ever been to (and I've been to many). My mind wasn't on the wedding though, it was elsewhere. I was happy for my family but I felt I did not fit in. Something was not right. My abusers were doing their bit - playing happy families with smiles on their faces. My husband knew I was not happy. He didn't have to ask me; he knows me well. My dad's brother was joking with his daughter as I was standing across from them. He was with his wife and kids, playing happy families. I had seen this many times before, but this time it was different.

My second abuser's wife was being nice to me also. She didn't normally really talk to me. To keep with the family tradition, she gave me a gift and some money. I had to accept this in front of everyone. I found this strange. For twenty years, she had not spoken to me, and all of a sudden, here she was, being nice to me-- something did not fit well, in my mind, but I was not to know the reason behind it at the time.

Then I found myself standing alone, with my second abuser close by. He was standing too near to me, with his elbow touching me. I quickly moved away and tried to forget it had happened. The wedding was over and it was time to go home. I was so glad I didn't have to stay any longer. We went to Mom's and got all our belongings together. My mom's house was full, as everyone had come to see my brother and his wife. We left after saying our goodbyes; I then went to see my cousin to say good-bye to her. I hugged her and was in tears. She knew what I had been through. I just wanted to release the emotions that I had inside me. She cried too, so I felt that she understood. We came back home and I felt comfortable again.

This was when things started to change for me. I was on the internet chatting to my cousin (My first abuser's daughter), and trying to organise my fortieth birthday party. I longed for that day, when all my family would come to my house. I had waited so long for this to happen. I wanted to show them 'yes your daughter, sister--she has made it'.

I had gained everything that I wanted in my life. I was complete and had accomplished my goal. I had a husband who adored me, and my two boys. As I was arranging the party, I had a niggling question that I did not know how to address. I was inviting all my family- aunties, cousins, nearly everyone, but I didn't know how to say that I did not want my two uncles there. How was I going to approach this subject? This particular cousin already knew about my second abuser, but I was not sure if she knew about her dad. I had always assumed she would have known, as my mom had told her mom when I was seventeen years old. I was quite sure her mom would have told her; after all, two girls living in the same house with an abuser should be aware of the situation. Surely her mother wanted to protect her girls; surely she would see that as part of a mother's role?

How wrong I was to assume that. As I was chatting excitedly to my cousin about my party, I said straight out that I didn't want her dad to attend. She asked me why. I paused, realising that she didn't know what had happened to me, but she persisted in asking me why so I decided to tell her. I wrote, 'because your dad abused me when I was three.' The internet went dead. What had I done? But there was relief and I started crying uncontrollably. My husband was asleep next to me. I woke him and told him what happened. He told me not to worry and gave me a hug.

I waited for two days but didn't hear from my cousin. She didn't come back on-line, or send me an e-mail. I sent one to her saying 'sorry, I thought you knew.' I got a reply from her telling me she hadn't known and that she wished I hadn't told her. I also contacted her older sister to ask for her help, as she had reassured me that she would be there for me if ever I needed her. I was wrong to take her at her word, as I got a very nasty email back from her.

I called my mom and told her I could not take it anymore, and I was going to tell my brothers and my sister. Mom begged me not to, as she said it would destroy the family. "You are married with children, just forget the past, leave it, as it is going to destroy lives and your brother has just got married," she said. I had heard this so many times before, and it had stopped me from going any further, but this time was different. I had taken just about enough from all of them and wanted to be at peace.

I e-mailed my three brothers, called my sister, and told them all. As I was speaking to my sister, I broke down in tears . The words just about came out. "Why do you think my uncles don't talk to me?" I asked her.

"Because you married a Muslim," she answered.

I then told her about the abuse that I had suffered over the years . My sister suffers from depression so I don't know how much it affected her, but from that day I never really heard from her again. This could be because she is married and her husband does not want her to be involved with me. I was made to believe I was the one at fault.

Never have I cried as much as I did that following week. My eyes felt as if they were popping out of their sockets, and were constantly sore and red. I pushed myself to get on with my duties as a wife, mother and employee. I drove to work with tears rolling down my cheeks. I felt such a mess. I informed the necessary people at work about what I was going through, and tried hard to focus on my job and my family. I forced myself to eat and did the best I could to look after myself. On one particularly bad day, I decided to come home early and phone a help line--the first time I had ever thought about doing so. As soon as someone answered, I started to cry uncontrollably. I told the lady on the phone what I had gone through. She just said one sentence: "It was not your fault."

Hearing those words released something deep inside me. I believed her and I listened to what she had to say. I was an emotional mess but at the same time, I was relieved. She was right. It wasn't my fault. All these years I had been made to believe I was the one to blame. Why had I been made to feel like that? I wondered. Maybe shutting me out made it easier for the family to cope with what had been done to me—easier to just ignore it.

This was the beginning of a new journey for me. Every time I told someone, it was such a relief, and I started to feel the burden lifting from my shoulders. I told everyone I could think of, and this prompted phone calls from my family. My auntie told me to stop this and if I didn't I would destroy my marriage. She said that the police will not listen to me as it was such a long time ago.

Then my cousin called me to offer his support, saying that this was my time and that he would help me. These phone calls continued for a week or two. I started to believe that my family was finally going to help me. I had no reason not to believe them. I told my family that I was going to the police to report my uncles. They asked me if it was worth it, telling me I would destroy families if I went ahead (including my marriage) but said that if I decided to go ahead, they would support me.

I was still scared at this stage, wondering if their predictions about my marriage would come true. My husband asked me one question: was it physical and emotional abuse? I said yes and his reply was that it wasn't my fault. Hearing this was such a relief and I just cried. He said he would back me all the way. I couldn't believe he was being so supportive. I wish I would have confronted my past sooner, so that, when I first met my husband, I would have been able me to move on as I now have. At the same time, I was thinking of my extended family. I didn't want to hurt them, as I do love them still. In the end, I had to put myself first, as I had already let go of the tension by telling everyone I was stress free. I had to get this right, as it was my past I had cried to the family for forty years for. This was my chance to tell everyone what I had gone through. I wanted to be free of the pain I had carried for forty years. It was no longer my secret: it now belonged to the family as I had done my fair share.

I went to the police and made a statement. As I had already let go of all the tension the disclosures I had made, I found making the statement stress- free. I had to get this right; This was my chance to tell my story like it was. I wanted to be free of all pain I had been carrying with me.

The police interview lasted three hours. I had made notes, as it was such a long time ago, and I was relieved to be allowed to take my notebook into the interview. The sergeant interviewing me had a very calming manner. When I had finished my statement, I began to feel at peace.

I had transferred the heavy burden I had carried for so many years onto someone else, and I was free of it. It now belonged to my brothers, sister, cousins, aunties and everyone else I told. There was no way I would ever take it back.

Meditations

ome weeks later, I picked up the phone to call Mom, as I did regularly, but the line was engaged. I decided to meditate while I was waiting. I had never tried meditation before. I closed my eyes, relaxed and thought of Mom's priest. What came next was unbelievable.

In my third eye, I saw a priest, but I couldn't see his face: all I could see was a man with a shawl. I opened my eyes and re-did the meditation. Again, I saw the same person. I called my mom and told her what had happened. She said I had her highest priest and not everyone sees him. I found out later that the highest priests don't show their faces. Mom was getting excited for me, saying that her priest was with me, and he would guide me. That evening I decided to have another go at meditation. Once again, many priests appeared before my eyes; colourful images of all the priests in the Indian community.

I would phone Mom regularly to tell her how I was getting on with my meditations and how I was feeling. What I heard next from her was shocking. I dismissed it, as I couldn't believe what she had just said. Perhaps her words came out wrong. She told me that she was beginning to love me. I didn't question her, as I think I was in shock.

In all these years, it never entered my head that my mom did not love me. I know we were not close because of my past, but I was not expecting her to say those words. I felt hurt and my heart was aching. I knew our relationship was different: I would watch my siblings hugging and kissing Mom, but could not bring myself to do the same. I often wanted to grab my mom and just tell her how much I loved her, but I couldn't. We hugged when we greeted each other and she hugged me back tightly. It never occurred to me that she didn't have any love for me.

To this day I continue to do my meditations. I have had so many spiritual experiences. It took me 40 years of heartache to get to where I am today. As my mind has become freed of my past, I have been able to concentrate more. I am taking it very slowly and don't know where I'm heading yet; I am just enjoying my meditations. I can hear music in my ears and whispers, but wherever the sounds are coming from, it's too far for me to see at the moment. I feel someone with me, andI don't know who it is, but they are making me feel so comfortable. I am just taking it very slowly though. I do my meditations every night. Five to ten minutes a day is enough and I'm so relaxed. I do them because I love doing it, not because I have to. I get the vibrations and first time I heard paper shuffling in my bedroom. The vibrations are really getting stronger. I lie with my legs flat on the floor and I feel a heavy presence of spirit in front of me. My body felt like a tree branch, rooted; this to me felt as if I were grounded and well-protected by the spirit world. Although my mind is still, I sometimes can't stop talking to whoever is with me. I know I shouldn't; but I can't help it. I do need to start listening to my thoughts, as I know that is where all the answers are. Last night I decided to sit on the floor and do my meditation. I was being rocked backward and forward, and it was a very nice feeling. This was the first time this had happened to me.

I wasn't going to meditate last night but thought what ten minutes is. So I did. I felt a very strong presence and was making my heart jump. I just panicked and came out of my meditation and it stayed with me. I was really panicking, and I asked my medium friend what had happened. They reassured me it was my guide getting me used to their presence. I am so glad that on this journey,

I have made some lovely friends who are there for each other. I feel I'm getting closer to meeting my guides and I'm taking it easy. I hope my experience will help others starting out.

When I meditate, I know someone is with me, but I don't know who it is yet. I asked a medium and she advised me to write some questions down and ask one question at a time until I got an answer. I did this Once I decided to try this, I didn't get an answer straight away, but a few hours later when I was in bed. I asked the question, "Who is with me?" I was shown a picture of my mom's higher priest. I doubt myself sometimes and I know I shouldn't. I did see him when I first started to meditate.

These are the questions that I had asked.

1: Who is with me?

2: What do you want?

3: Where do I go from here?

I try to meditate in the evenings at a regular time. This is mine and the spirit world's time, and they know when it's our time together.

I was meditating today, and I didn't get anything, but was brought out of my concentration because my phone rang. When I looked at the time, I found I had been meditating for an hour. I know I didn't fall asleep; rather, meditation is when spirit is working on my soul.

Last night I couldn't sleep around 1 o'clock in the morning. So I decided to do another meditation. I found I was really scared and I did my grounding and protective bubble. Someone was with me to my left by the door. I have had this experience before, where there is another force beside me. I had to stop for a time, as this really frightened me, but over the years I have learned to love my fear. To this day I have no fear, and so to this day, I continue with my meditations and thoroughly enjoy them.

A simple meditation that I use:

1. Sit comfortably in a chair in a quiet room.
2. Breath in and out slowly-this can take a few minutes.
3. Breathe negative out and positive in.
4. Clear your mind of all the daily activities.
5. Focus on an object in your third eye-I use a good memory, or it could be a lit candle.
6. Then just relax and see what you get.
7. For the first time, I suggest you only do it for five minutes.
8. Then slowly bring you self out.
9. You should feel relaxed.

I hope this exercise helps you and it relaxes you.

The Investigation:

It is MY Time Now

n due course, the police began gathering statements from the list of contacts I gave them. My cousin had said it was my time for help, so I was shocked when I found out he didn't want to speak to the police. I didn't call anybody or pressure anyone. I always believed God was with me and, as long as I did the right thing, nothing else mattered.

Then I found out Mom didn't want to go to the police station to give her statement. That was hurtful, as I didn't really expect that from her. I was in tears. She was my mother and I needed her. Why wasn't she there for me, when I needed her the most? Everyone else I could live without but this was my mother. As the case steadily progressed, she did in time agree to speak to the police. Her words were "As I gave birth to you, I will do this for you". I thanked her, and then asked myself why I was saying thank you to my mother. This was the least she could do, and I wish now she had helped me years ago, when I had desperately needed her to. Why did she imply that I should be grateful to her for supporting me, her daughter? Didn't she know what she was saying was destroying me inside? I was hurting but I kept it inside, as I had done for so many years.

After she gave her statement, I discovered that she had held back from telling the police everything that she knew relating to my case. Again, in disbelief, I realised that my family were not doing or saying enough, despite their promises to support me. I was doing all I could to bring my abusers to face up to what they had done...I believed I deserved that. I didn't deserve those who had promised to walk with me turning their back on me at the time I needed them most.

But they will have to live with the guilt for the rest of their lives. I will be free forever, free from the burden that has weighed heavily on my heart.

My mom was starting to open up to me now. She told me they found out about my uncle abusing me at the age of four. By doing nothing, they made me suffer in silence. All for family honour, because my grandmother had asked her to forgive her son. My mom said she was the only one who expressed anger towards my uncle- no one else stood with her and supported her in that way.

My dad's brothers and their wives knew, but they did nothing. I therefore grew up completely unaware that they all knew. No one wanted to support my mom, so she in turn felt powerless to help me. No-one kept an eye on me and made sure I was safe; I carried on living in the same house as my abuser; seeing him every day and night. I was constantly frightened that they would leave me alone in his presence. I was so glad when my dad bought us our own house--but it was just next door. At least I was out of that house, although I still had to face him every day. Where was my dad in all this and why did he not protect me, his little girl? The answer to this is that he was never around - it was left to Mom to bring us up. There is no love lost between dad and me.

I would call Mom two to three times a week as I was getting excited about opening up to God. After each experience, I would call her. One morning a woman in spirit showed herself to me, and spoke to me. Her words were: "Love yourself." I did not know what she meant at the time.

Eventually, I realised what she meant and I do love myself every day. There is always a smile on my face and I am so proud of myself. I have had spirits show me many wonderful things and I look forward to a future with these spirits; I feel so lucky that they have chosen me to come to. That to me means that spirit has accepted me. I sense many presences around me, but don't know how to communicate with the spirit world yet. I am just happy to have them with me, as I know they are helping me in my journey ahead.

The Outcome

y case didn't get to court, as no-one in the family stood by me. I was upset for a day or so, but then I started to think. At the end of all this sorrow, I gained a very big gift, which was the hand of God. Not everyone can say that they have found God-- but I did.

I live my life as a very happy woman who has everything she can possibly desire. Nobody in the family talks to me, but I call Mom sometimes. Even then, it's usually a short conversation, but when we talk about God, it can go on for an hour. In the end, I learned a very big lesson: the love of my family was all false love. There was no real love coming from them; it was all just to keep me sweet so I would not say anything.

Family will make you believe that they love you and that they understand. Deep down, they just wanted the shame of the abuse I had suffered to go away, and hoped that I was weak, and would keep my silence. But I became strong enough to speak up, and in doing so, have found my inner peace.

The little girl inside me, the inner me, has come out and it is up to me to free her fully. It wasn't her fault, and I have to let her know that there are no secrets. It is my responsibility to take care of her, and I will help her.

I close my eyes, and hold out my hand, to reach her hand. I

hold it tight and will never let it go again; it is my responsibility to look after her. By just talking to my inner child and telling her this, I will take the pain away. She wants to be free of all this hurt. If you have suffered too in this way, you need to be in charge too; you have to help this little girl, tell her in your mind not to be scared and that you are here to protect her. Hold her hand tight, tighter and never let it go again. Send her lots of unconditional love. Tell her that you love her; that you will always be there for her, and will never let go of her hand. It is your duty as her owner, to be responsible for her.

The elders in my family had a responsibility for this little girl; the girl they forgot. They will have to suffer with their guilt for rest of their lives. I can continue on my spiritual path, because I have done the right thing. Mom has said sorry to me for not showing me love. This made me feel uncomfortable, because saying sorry is not something you expect from your mom. She has said she doesn't blame me but I know deep down she doesn't understand. I encouraged her to get counselling for herself so that she might get more understanding, and she did have one session with a councillor but she couldn't open up. It is going to eat her up inside if she continues carrying the burden and doesn't let it go.

My family are very religious. They worship their religion, with love and passion. They do the duties expected of them. They would give up their lives for the one who has been chosen as their leader, whom I have had the honour of meeting. I wrote him a letter asking for help, and was very surprised not to receive a letter or a phone call back. For someone who believes in God, and has thousands of followers, I was disappointed that they offered no help. It is such a big organisation, so surely, you would have people working for you who you could call on to help someone in need? I am still trying to get my head around this.

How can you believe in God, and at the same time, not do the right thing? I also believe in God, and I would never turn my back on someone who asked for my help. I do not understand why they would not want to help their daughter, because that is what I am to them.

Forgiveness

n order for me to forgive, this is something I will never forget. To gain my inner peace; to move forward, think positive and be strong to help others, I felt I had to forgive. It has made me stronger and more powerful as a person. How the offenders move on from this is up to them, as they have to live with their conscience. Now that it is out in the open, they have nothing to hide behind.

Forgiveness plays a big part in gaining your inner peace. You have to let go of your past and move on with the life you have now. You will feel it in yourself when you are ready to forgive. Only do it when you actually feel that you can. I would have never forgiven, until I found out that CPS wasn't going to take my case on. I was distraught. I sat down and cried. I felt let down by family, and then the system. I cried for a few days and then thought, prior to all this happening. In that year, my spiritual side opened up more. I saw spirit, lights in my bedroom wall. When I meditated, I felt my aura all around me. I am never alone. I have my spirit guide with me, trailing an aroma which smells of violet and very sweet. Then there are other guides around me. I truly felt in my heart God held my hand and I know I work for him.

Although our destiny was written by God before I was born, He also gave us free will. With that free will, we humans can change our path. Alternatively, others can alter it to suit them.

Those others, in my case were my abusers. They changed my path. Do you see why I can forgive? I never ever hold a grudge and I send love to my enemies. When my uncles were being questioned, in my mind I was giving them strength to tell the truth. Only you will know when the time is right to forgive. Do not let your abuser be in control of your life. You are in charge of your body and soul. It belongs to you alone - do not let anyone make you believe otherwise. Forgive and move on and although you are forgiving in your mind, the abusers don't need to know. Let them think whatever they want to think.

I have also forgiven my family for the wrong done to me. I told them repeatedly what was happening to me. Even when I found out no one was going to help me with my case, I told my mom I would not pester them as God is on my side. They will have to live with the burden and the knowledge that they didn't do the right thing. They will not be at peace, while I have found mine. So I would say forgive, and although you will never forget what happened, in time, it does get easier, and you do get your life back.

I want to say to all victims out there: you, too, can achieve this inner peace. Be strong, brave and take the first step and, in the end, you will be the winner. Moving from victim to survivor is overwhelming and feels like magic. You will feel the inner peace in you when you speak, breathe; and you will become a new person.

Be positive and love yourself, as you are special and God loves you. You were given a path in this lifetime, but with the free will of others, you were taken off that path. Now that you are back on your path, enjoy what was planned for you before you were born. All those tears that you have shed have given you healing powers which you can now use to heal others. I feel my role in this world now is that I am working with God.

God will be with me for the rest of my living days. I have walked my path; I am waiting for my next task in life, and will take it on happily. Whilst I am writing this, I have a big smile on my face, which will stay with me forever.

Life truly does get better. Peace within is found again.

Poems

have found that inner peace within, so powerful strong and yet so calming. I nearly lost it but with strength and support, I found it again.

Throughout my ordeal, I have become a stronger person.

It all started when I turned 40, when I decided that my past needed to stay in my past. I put pen to paper and started to write poems after a friend had told me "write down your feelings in a poem".

I had never written poems in my life, but that is just what I did and from that day on, in fact, I could not stop. I would get a thought in my head, along would come the feelings, and the words would just flow. Some of the poems are sad, because sometimes that was how I was feeling at the time. I am not that sad person anymore as with time I have been able to let go of the past, gradually changing and becoming stronger, I am a happy person who is now content with her life. I have everything that I could ever want, a wonderful husband and two lovely boys, a network of friends and handful of family members who I love dearly.

I have decided to share some of my poems with you and sincerely hope you enjoy reading them as much as I enjoyed writing them. Every time I look back and read my poems I have a cry. I can't help it as they did start off being very sad. Towards the end, they do become happy and I began to have a smile on my face.

My Life and Good Bye Tears

As I, sit here wondering what life is going to throw next at me,
I look back at my life and think what if I did that this way
Would my life have been a bit different and maybe easier?
I don't think it would have been made any simpler;
This is what my life was going to be like.
Maybe now that all the bad times have passed,
Maybe I can start to enjoy my life a bit more;
But why can't I enjoy my life the way I want to
Why is it I am living my life the way someone else wants me to?
It's my life and I want it back, as it belongs to me
Where did my strength come from when I was fighting to put my
past right?
Where has that strength gone, now that I want to sort my present
out?
The tears came back to me, as if to say, "we are still here."
They felt like old times, as if they never left me.
I don't want to go to that awful place again;
I am going to fight for what I believe in,
As it's my life and I want to reclaim it back.
Looks like I have another fight on my hands.
Well I am good at fighting back--and I will.

They Wanted a Girl

Born in a family where they wished for a girl,
Was there much happiness when I came?
Celebrations, when I was born:
I was the daughter they longed for.

Daughter, whom they loved and forgot
They didn't look after me well at all.
Where were they when I was hurting?
Not one of them was there.

Just wanted you to hold my hand,
Hold me; don't take your eyes off me.
It's me, the daughter you longed for--
You did look away didn't you?
Your hand nowhere to be seen,
I was left again to defend for myself.

I couldn't, though; I was three,
All on my lonesome, I was to be
Suffering in silence, this was your daughter,
Daughter you longed for--
You did take your eyes off of me, didn't you?

Made to Watch

Was three and made to watch;
Didn't understand what was happening,
There were no cries, just silence.
Told her in my teens I knew
How could you, as you were three?
I saw what happened to you.
She went quiet as I spoke;
Didn't talk about it again,
Was it the end of that conversation?

Didn't Want to Go

Didn't want to go;
at the same time, felt left out--
Watched everyone go,
Stayed by myself;
But tears were with me,
So I was not alone.
Was all in my thoughts--
Wasn't I part of them?
Wanted to fit in so much;
Burned with love for them;
So wanted to be with them,
but I had to be the strong one.
It was safe to stay away;
They all returned home,
Not a thought for me.
I was left in my world all alone;
No one knew why I was like this.
I was safe that day;
Don't know about other days.
We will see if I cannot go,
As I like the feeling of being free--
That wasn't to be.
I was the one chosen to experience this pain;
This was my destiny.

Confused and Lost in My World

Confused and lost in my world
Looked at other girls I did
Wondered if they were like me
Couldn't just be me could it
Was I that special girl?
There was no talk on this
No one said anything
Therefore, I did not ask questions;
Just carried on with life,
As numb as I could.
Why didn't my voice shout out,
"I am here; help me please?"
It is because I knew there was no help;
Already had asked and no one came,
Would tell someone and never see them again.

Maybe it was all my doing for being pretty?
I was to blame; I did this to me--
Why was I so pretty and innocent?
Didn't help me, being like that--
Would have liked to experience ugliness,
Then maybe I wouldn't have got a looking.
I could have experienced a happy childhood;
That would have been nice.
No--then, I wouldn't be me.
Had to experience this pain
In order to be the person I became;
One with a beautiful heart,
With so much love to give.

Suffering in Silence I Was

Suffered in silence, all alone I felt;
Crying into my pillow, no one heard.
Plucked up the courage to tell all;
'we already know,' was the answer;

That's where it was left again.
No one came back to me;

a hug would have been nice--
was left again to my suffering.
All alone, no one to talk to, again:
Just me, my thoughts and tears.
No one cared, or did they?

There were no cuddles, no words of comfort;
No time when someone held my hand

to say 'it's going to be okay,'
Someone has held my hand now;
Will never let it go again—never,
As it's going to be ok now--I know.

Can't do this Any More

Sat there saying, "I can't do this,"
Let me be free and fly away,
Like the bird in the sky.
Then there were those tears,
Not on me they were
I kept feeling, asking, why am I doing this,
Why was I feeling the hurt?
I want to be that bird
Who can reach up to the sky.
Go higher and higher;
Never to return again
Then I will be free again
That wasn't to be
Wasn't my time to fly?
Will be one day;
That day is not now--
But it will be soon.

Engaged at Seventeen

Got engaged at seventeen--
This was my way out.
That's what I thought anyway;
Had no feelings for him; none.
He was my escape from all this pain,
Couldn't go through with it in the end
How was I going to get out of this, then?
Plucked up the courage to tell them,
Didn't want to marry him, I said
They weren't happy with that.
In end, I told them the reason why.
No help was offered, none at all
It was left at that;and that was that--
What is left to say, then?

Their family honour was at stake;
Didn't realise then, but yes that was the way.
Had to protect sisters, brothers and cousins
Who would hate them if they all knew
I couldn't take any more; it was too much for me.
Pills didn't taste nice; no they didn't--
But that was the only choice I could see.
They found me in time; yes they did--
Still there was none of that help.
Didn't have to marry him in the end, but I was
Still stuck in my suffering,
All alone; deep in thought--
the thought that one day I would be free.

Booked a ticket so could fly away

Wanted to escape far away;
Fly with the wind higher and higher.
I had no wings of my own;
Booked a ticket to go away,
Never to return back again.
I got my ticket and held it tight,
New York was my destination--
That was far away wasn't it?
I waited for my plane to take me away;
Sat there thinking of my family,
and missing them already.
I wasn't brave enough, though;
I started to panic and think,
So I phoned my friend to meet me.
She came and just took me to her place,
No questions asked as to why.
That's when I started to rebuild my life--
my life, which was in pieces.

Got myself together as best I could;
That's what I thought anyway.
I wasn't alone; my tears were still on my journey--
They weren't ready to leave just yet.
My family did find me at my new place
I thought I was well hidden
"We missed you," they said with tears.
"I'm not coming back home now," I told them,
"This is where I have made my life,
"Free of the pain you couldn't save me from.
No memories are here with me to think about."
That's what I told them, as it was easier for me.
"You can stay here, but keep in touch," they said;
That's what I did--stayed in touch and kept their honour.
I still wasn't free to fly away; I stayed instead.
I hope that I was the daughter they wanted me to be.

Held head up high

I attended most family functions;
Head held high, as to say "I am brave,"
I showed no emotions or tears.
I was their elder daughter;
Did everything expected of me, though tears
were at the back of my eyes,
Wasn't going to show them
They weren't going to see me down.
That's what they would have wanted;
To see me break down and cry.
Held my husband's hand and showed them.
There was no eye contact;
I did my elder daughter's duties,
No one really knew the truth.
I kept their family honour,
Which they loved so dearly
Didn't really understand why
I kept it together for them
As this was my duty as a daughter
That's what I thought anyway.

Called Mom Regularly

Would call Mom regularly,
"Do something please,
Your daughter is hurting
I have so much pain.
My heart hurts when I breathe,
Ease this pain I'm carrying."
"Not today," was always the reply,
"Good bye." Mom will call again.
Every weekend was my time with Mom;
Again, the same request: help me.
"Was your fault," those are the words Mom would use;
I believed those words, I did.
Maybe it was all my doing,
Still phoned and asked for help;
Thought one day she might.

Watched Them do Their Duties

Would watch them doing their duties
With their families standing by their side;
They were well respected by all.
Only I and a handful of family members knew the real truth;
I was brave to stand there,
Brave and strong, that was me
Inside I was hurting and torn,
wanted to shout and scream,
but something was holding me back.
Was it what the elders were saying--
"Keep our family honour,
Not everyone needs to know"?
Just watched their happy faces--
That's what I thought anyway.

Met Someone I Liked

I met someone I liked;
Our eyes did click--
Never spoke to him though.
Asked my family," will he do?"
A quick no was the reply.
I asked my brother too:
"He's well-educated, and not for you."
Left it that way, hurting inside--
the next day met my husband-to-be:
He said it was love for him.
Then someone I liked wanted to see me;
"Too late now," I said with hurt,
"Met someone else I have."
My husband is my other soul--
We did get married,
It was meant to be--
Married, but not in my home town;
This was not allowed.
What would people say?
Couldn't invite everyone;
Could not be done,
As everyone would ask questions.
Kept my family honour once again,
Had my small wedding--
A happy, sunny day it was, but
Deep down wanted my big wedding.
Wasn't to be in this lifetime.
No, it wasn't to be.

Not Coming to Your Funeral when You Die

Pass a message to granddad --
"I'm not coming to your funeral.
I know you will pass over soon;
I tried so hard to talk to you.
Gave up after 20 years;
That was enough of trying--
Couldn't waste any more time.
I knew you were stubborn
Like me in a way, in the end;
Don't know if you got the message--
Was anyone brave enough to give it?
I was already at your house,
When you decided your time was up--
Did you wait for me to be there?

I wouldn't have come otherwise
I saw you in your coffin all at peace;
Peace, which you didn't make with me.
Deep down, you really loved me:
I know that you did, as I was your girl.
Heard your voice in my ear, one morning,
calling someone else and not me.
You always said that, didn't you ?
There was no mention of me; none.
I was first born but not first choice
I do and will always love you ;
You were and always will be my Granddad .
I don't mind coming second best--
Well, I wasn't that either, was I?

My Grandmother

Then there was my grandmother
Loved her more than anyone
We had a strong bond
Thinking about it now
Is it because she new
That's way she showed me love
Cried for months when she went
Always in my mind and heart
I have learned that she also new
She has become a distant thought
Now that is very sad
I loved my grand mother
Why did she do that to me?
Thought she loved me
I still love her I do
Can't stop loving her now

Something to Tell You

She came to me tears pouring down her cheeks
I got something to tell you she said
Lost someone in the night
No words would come out
Just said ,"oh I'm sorry,"
She couldn't get her breath
All tears she was
What do you say when you have lost a loved one
Gave her a hug nearly in tears
Held my tears in as it wasn't my time to cry
But to support her
Will be back in a few weeks she said,
Take your time to heal
It will get better in time, and you will heal.

Lived a Positive Life

Lived a positive life and did my best
Did good in everything I touched
Smiled and sent love to all
Deep down I was in pieces
Gave out love got lots of love back
This was nice I thought to myself
No, it was all false as there was no love
It was to keep me sweet
So I would keep quiet
I believed those lies
I was in pain
But I kept my secret; I did
There honour was safe for now.

Close My Eyes and Look Back

I close my eyes and look back
Taking pill after pill after pill
Cutting deeper and deeper
Enjoying the pain as it gave me relief
For a second I could forgot
Feeling numb and free of this hurt
No matter how hard I try
Memory's still within so deep
Pills cutting they didn't work
Was still alive and feeling pain
It wasn't the time for it to leave
This pain I had to experience
Few more years before I am free
Can be waiting a lifetime
Will it be today tomorrow?
No, it's not my time to be free
Will wait patiently in pain
I can take this; I'm brave.

Why Didn't They Help?

Why didn't they help when I told them?
I did tell them and they did know
What was going through their minds?
Was it there honour and the shame it will be
I know it wasn't for their daughter
Told them with tears pouring down my cheeks
They could have stopped this carrying on
No one came back to me to say it's going to be ok
Continued in silence with my suffering
I'm getting good at this hurt and pain
I will keep their family honour safe
For now anyway, as I'm not strong.

Told Their Mom 'Look After Your Girls'

Told their mom look after your girls
I wasn't safe once upon time
That was me this is your time
You look after your girls
Don't leave them alone
They need their mom
I couldn't be saved
You save your girls
I know you can't leave
You have to protect your honour
We will do it together
Will keep silent so you can live your life
Just look after your girls
I have told you what happened
It's up to you, as I am weak.

Life Truly Does Begin at 40

Longed for family to come home

They never came to my house

All those years had passed

Decided to celebrate my birthday, Yes that was my 40th; the big one

The one that says life begins at 40, I was not to know how true that was

Had to experience it for myself

That's when my life changed, Started to tell everyone and all

This is what happened to me, Elders would say don't do it

You will truly be the loser, I didn't listen; I kept shouting

To whoever would listen to me?

Need to tell you something, they did listen and in shock

I was all tears and all emotional, Never felt like this in 40 years

That was the worst ever for me

It was my time to release to the world, Bit by bit I felt free of this burden

It wasn't my pain any more

I am free and can fly away

Have returned the pain to its rightful owner

Carrying it for so long for you

You can experience for yourself how I felt

I have no pain--just love to show.

Past Coming to an End

Everything happens for a reason
I chose this life before I was born
I must have wanted to experience tears
Oh and I sure got loads of tears
Why am I feeling those tears again
Its because it took me forty years to put it right
Know that I am doing the right thing it hurts
I know now that it wasn't my fault
Why didn't anyone help when I was crying to them
It doesn't matter now, as I'm sorting it out myself
When this is all over I don't want any more tears
I want to experience what it's like to be happy
Will my family forgive me for standing up for myself?
I had to fight for myself and I hope to win the battle
I do very much miss my family
Come from a big family and still feel alone,
I can feel my happiness returning
These tears will fade slowly.

Crying Out for Help but No One is Listening

I'm crying out for help please support me
Not one person is listening to me
I'm shouting to everyone and all
Maybe out of the hundreds one might shout back
Here's hoping I might get lucky if I carry on shouting
But why is no one listening to me
I'm the one who needs the support now
I have been keeping quiet for so long
Can't keep protecting all and everyone
This is my last chance to have my say
This is my turn to say it's my turn help me
All I ask is the truth to come to the surface
Why is everyone so scared of the truth
This has made me such a strong person
I am so ready to take them all on
They are they not so strong like me
Why are they so scared of the truth
Truth will and always will come out
Why is everyone ignoring my cries
I pray every night for strength and support
To help me win my battle that I have started
Please listen to my cries I need you at this time
Please give me the strength to continue with my fight,
I can't break down now
I've got a happy ending waiting for me.

Did have a Big Family; What Happened

When I was born, I had such a big family
I would say there were hundreds of them
One by one, they became a distant thought
I ended up with a handful of family members
who were not from the time I was born
They are my new family that I have made
Out of the hundreds, I thought loved me
One by one, they all disappeared nowhere to be seen
What did I do to deserve all this sorrow?
I loved those hundred family members
I will always love them forever and ever
The time has come to say my goodbyes
To all those hundred family members
I will always love you all and you will be forever in my heart
I know I am a distant memory to you all;
But I have my handful of family members who love me for what I
have become;
They have never and never will judge me like you all did
My life is changing forever and ever
No more going back; only forward.

When's All this Going to End

Suddenly think it's getting better
Life is finally where it should be
No more of that sadness
Everything going to plan
God finally held my hand
Then suddenly a bomb shell
Your back to where you started
Mom is the one you trust most
Well you should trust Mom shouldn't you
Then why is it that I feel I have no mom
Mom chooses others before her own blood
I said I wasn't going to cry any more
Wish I could believe those words
Someone tell me it's going to be okay
Cant go back to where I started from
Want to leave my past in the past
It doesn't belong in the future now
I was on the right track, I thought
Will see what tomorrow brings
Happiness--I hope.

Why Didn't My Mom Love Me?

Why didn't my mom love me?
It wasn't my fault
I didn't ask for this to happen
All I wanted was a hug
Mom has realised that now
Mom is starting to love me again
Oh god it feels good
Can feel that warmth
Still there are no hugs
As we are so faraway
Mom, please come home
and give me a hug.

Why am I Feeling Like This?

Feelings I thought I had dealt with
They appear again and in more ways;
When is all this going to be over?
My tears are caught inside my head;
My stomach is physically feeling sick
One of me and lots of them--
Family, why did you not help then?
Now that I'm doing something myself,
Still no help from them--
Why do I feel so alone?
How am I going to get my justice?
Everyone is thinking of themselves;
Did I miss my turn for help

When is it my time?
I am feeling for my mom;
No one gave her the correct advice.
Hope it's not too late to get Mom back;
Someone, please make her understand.
Please, all I ask is she be healed
She has had to put up with lots of pain
Because she gave birth to me
I now it was my destiny that it was to be.
Why put my mom through all this
She didn't deserve to be part of it
I would have been strong for both
Take tears, sickness, worried feelings away
I want to be the happy me again
Please make this go away

So Mom could see her girl is happy and free--

So she could sleep with peace.

Phoned a Stranger

All these years, I never felt like this
I was such an emotional mess
I had cried before; but not like this .
Called for some advice;
Cried my heart out to a stranger--
"It wasn't your fault," she said.
Hearing those strong words
Made me cry even more
I believed this stranger
This made me fight even more
So I did fight back--
This was the beginning.

They Said it's YOUR Time Now

Everyone was calling me
Didn't stand with you when you needed us most
This is your time and we will help you
Well that's what they said
And I believed those lies
Every other day I would get a call
We want to stand with you
You have been so brave
By keeping our family honour
Felt I had family who cared for me
They said they were going to help me be free
How wrong was I to believe them?
When it came down to telling the truth
No one held my hand to say "We will help,"
I was left all alone again, deep in thought
Will fight myself I can do this
I did fight back but lost everyone
But gained my peace within.
That's all I ever wanted:
My peace and me.

My Rock

He is my rock; my husband.

One question he asked me,

I told him the answer:

"Wasn't your fault," he said.

Tears rolled down my cheeks; for me to hear those words

Made me want even more to fight.

He is the one who stood by me, when no one else was brave
enough.

He is the one that gave me the strength

He will always be my rock, in everything that I do and will do:

Love you so much Hun bun.

They Have Been Told the Outcome

They have been told the outcome; they will have to live with this
Nowhere and no one to hide behind
I can look up and walk with my head held up high
They will be looked at forever, for the rest of their living days
I did what was right, my conscience is clear
They will never be at peace; I have gained my inner peace
I can move on with my life
Most lovely, happy life that I have made for me.

Can't Find Strength to Phone Mom

Can't find strength to phone Mom;
What am I going to say?
How do I tell her I had to do this?
This was my journey on this path. If I didn't do this, it would have
Been waiting in my next life, Couldn't go through this pain again
This was meant to be
Mom will understand
Will she? Hope she will.

Not My Pain Take it Away

Sit here thinking no more
Taking away Mom's pain
Want to live my life know
It's my time not Mom's
Mom was given chance to put it right
She chose others before her flesh
It's my time to move on and I will
It's my time to enjoy this time
My time to live a happy life
That's what I will do now
No more of this pain
It's not my pain; its Mom's
I will be fine; I will.

Phoned Mom and Told her the Outcome

Phoned mom and told her the outcome
Mom, it wasn't written in my destiny to fight
I am honestly and truly good within
If they were locked up, they would truly be free
True winner is me, as they will have to face the world
I did everything possible that was expected of me
Won't look back and say I didn't do that this way or that way
Mom don't be upset; I'm still your little girl
Will always be that little girl you gave birth to
Your little girl, only yours and no one else's
We will celebrate our new birth again
No more tears please; no more tears
This is the end of the road for our fight
Lets forgive and move on, as it wasn't to be
Send them love they didn't know what they were doing
This is truly our win as it has brought us closer
We can find that love that we lost all those years ago
I did lose my mom all those years ago
But I have found you once again;
Please don't leave me again.
I need my mom; I will always need you, Mom.

This was how I felt when I had My Boys

The moment I saw you gazing into my eyes
Oh what warmth I felt from you
You had your eyes wide open
This was the moment I first saw you.
You were my special little boys
There were none of those tears
Then you smiled at me;
I knew then that I was going to have
more of those special moments

Maybe I could put my past to rest

New beginnings with you

I know it wasn't to be;

It wasn't your fault--

You did heal me a little bit.

Thinking NO More Pain

Sit here thinking no more
Taking away Mom's pain
Want to live my life now
It's my time, not Mom's
Mom was given a chance to put it right;
She chose others before her flesh
It's my time to move on and I will
It's my time to enjoy this time
My time to live a happy life
That's what I will do know
No more of this pain
It's not my pain; its Mom's
I will be fine, I will.

Kids Playing will I be Safe Tonight

I look at my kids happily playing
They look so innocent, they do
Not a care or thought in the world
Then I look back at my childhood
My siblings playing; not a care at all
I was playing too-- but there was a thought
Am I going to be safe this time, at night
I won't be too innocent then, will I?
I play with siblings with fear and pain
Oh I wish I wasn't in pain--so much pain
I want my time back, want to be like my kids
Kids, Mom will protect you to the day I die
You are my innocent lads, mine all mine
My responsibility, all mine--I will protect you

Your mom is here and always will be.

Your Big Sister was Lost in World of her Own

My brothers I love dearly, I do love you all
Mom, I promise I will look after them
Big sister was lost in world of her own
Big sister is once again found
Brothers have got their big sister back
I promise, Mom I will look after them
They are my responsibility now
Leave them to me, Mom
I will take care of them, I will
It's my duty to do that;
I am their big sister, after all.

Asked Husband a Question

I asked my husband a question
Am surprised at the answer
He is changing with me, he is
He listens while I talk, he does
About my newfound knowledge,
Whereas in the past he would pretend
He is learning with me, he is
My newfound knowledge
Together we can experience
This newfound happiness
Love you, my lovely hubby, love you
We are truly soul mates, we are.

Memory's Packing Suitcase

One memory I have
Packing my suitcase
nine or ten I was, then
Where are you going?" asked a voice
"Nowhere," I said, "nowhere."
In my mind, I wanted to disappear
Nowhere to be seen again
That wasn't going to happen
Stuck in the same place
For ever and ever I was
Felt like that, it did
Someone rescue me; rescue me
I wasn't rescued; no I wasn't
I had to close my eyes and pretend;
Pretend it wasn't happening
Someone will rescue me, I hope.

Everything Happens for a Reason

In life everything happens for a reason
It all starts to click in place one day
All that we have and gone through life
There is a reason it all happens
We need to link and connect it together
All we meet in life, it slots into place
There's a reason why we met that person
The answer you get later on in life
That person comes back in your life again
To give you the answer that you wait for
The answer that you didn't get earlier when you met.

You will be Sent Strangers in Life

You will be sent strangers in life to you
They are sent by God for you with love
Accept them as they will need help
All they will ever need is your time
Only five minutes is enough to give
Give them your love with open arms
Your duty know that you have found God
You are his helper and you must do his work
Stand beside God and say, "I will help you"
Please send me strangers as I have lots of love;
Lots of love to give; I have lots of love.

Love Yourself She Said

Love yourself she said
That was her message
She flashed in front of my face
Dark silky hair Black it was tan face
That was the first spirit that spoke to me
What a shock never seen before
Didn't know what she meant then
I do now, I sure do know
I love myself everyday
Will do for the rest of my days
I am special wonderful
All in one Yes all in one
I love what I became
New me is here forever and ever
I love me; yes I love me, I do.

What am I Going to do When Mom Goes

What am I going to do when mom goes
She will go one day she will--I know she will.
How do you show Mom love how
I have not done love with Mom;
Don't know how to do that.
Never kissed Mom ; not even on the cheek
Would love to hold Mom and give her a kiss,
Don't know how to do that, I don't know
She doesn't know either ;we are the same
I was first born, but not shown how to love;
Celebrated when I was born, they did
Although I was a daughter and not a son
That was then, they gave out sweets
Don't do that for girls I was told, no not for girls
I was special to them then, I was special
No more celebrations now
On my own again, and no Mom
Maybe we will learn how to love again
Hope so would love to know the feeling
Feeling how to love your mom
Must be a nice feeling, Yes it must.

That Little Voice Inside You will get Bigger

Yes that little voice inside you will get bigger
Will not stay faint and small for ever
You would have tried it but was faint
One day that voice will be heard yes it will
In the past you would have tried to make it bigger
But it wasn't your time and you wasn't strong
Know that you have found that voice oh yes
Does feel good when you can shout, doesn't it
They can say don't shout but you will
As its your time to be heard yes it is
This is your time yours to be heard
You make sure no one and no one says no
Use that bigger voice; it's your bigger voice for keeps.

So Much Love for Strangers

So much love for strangers
That's what I do all day long
Feels so good happy feeling inside
Why didn't I get this before?
Missed a lifetime of giving love
This is my time to give now;
Sure have lots to give.
I smile all day with strangers ;
They give smiles back freely
Feels so good to receive.
Tears of happiness I have;
Eyes shining with love
Long may this feeling last
As I have lots of love to give;
Will carry on giving love to strangers.

So Much Happiness in the World

So much happiness in the world
Then there is sadness yes sadness
We show a happy face, but inside we're sad
It's not easy to show feelings
We must learn to show more
More we show more we get back
Yes, the more we give the more we receive.

Feeling this Sadness Again

Why am I feeling this sadness again?
Is it the words Mom said last night?
"Sorry I couldn't show you my love,"
Don't be sorry; it wasn't meant to be
"Its our time now, we can learn how to love,"
"Don't be a stranger," she said; a stranger
"Everything will sort itself out, it will;
This will always be your home,
As long as Mom is here it will be."
"Mom, I won't be coming back home."
"Don't say that," she said,
"This is your home; your home."

No More Tears

No more tears please
you don't belong in this lifetime
you have overstayed your stay
It's time to say goodbye
Go back to where you belong
It isn't your time now;
you have done your job;
your time has expired.
Please leave now ,please
Goodbye, tears. Goodbye.

Why do We Choose to Live this Life?

Why do we choose to live this life?
Who's idea was it to make it so painful?
Why didn't we pick a life where there was just love;
No, that would have been too easy
If I had chosen a easier life, there would have been no tears

Forty years of tears were sad but at the same time, so healing
Why can't I cry anymore?
No more tears left in me;
Used up all my tears I have.
It's because I have healed, isn't it?
Where have those lovely tears gone?
I do miss them, as they were part of me.

Thank You

Thank you for making me the person I am today.
It was you who showed me how to feel pain;
It was the pain and hurt you gave.
It was you who made me this person;
I am what you made of me--
That sad, scared person

I have used those feelings to my advantage
In my life that I hold dearly now
I have forgiven and moved on with life
I survived; you lost. I won this fight;
I am a survivor--a survivor.

Still Feeling Tears

Why am I still feeling tears
Is there something I have missed
Feeling choked and in pain
Heart is hurting; can't breathe
I am a survivor; I have won
so, why am I still feeling this pain?
What am I missing here?
Will sit down and I'll think
Maybe it will come back to me
Oh it has, it's because Mom's still in pain
She blames herself; she couldn't help her little girl.
It wasn't her fault; she didn't have the support--
She can't find her inner peace.
Mom, you will be fine in time
I have forgiven you; I don't blame you.
Please, please find your inner peace
So I can be free of this pain I feel.

Want to Feel Inner Peace

I once said,"I want to feel that inner peace"
"You'll get that when you pass over to the other world,"

was the answer I got in return.
I am so glad I don't have to wait for that time.
As I have got my inner peace in this lifetime.
I'll tell her I have found my inner peace
Don't have to wait; I am alive and I have found peace.

This is How Life Should Be

Feeling happy life is how it should be
Mind you it took forty years
To get to where I am now
I have no quarrels
This is how I was going to get here
Had to take the long road
Now that I am here
There is no going back
This feelings are here to the end of my days.

Felt so much love for God today

Felt so much love for God today
Couldn't stop myself from smiling
Kept making mistakes as I was so in love
Felt so calm and full of joy
How did I get to this wonderful stage?
Didn't know this sort of feeling was within me
Feelings took so long for it to surface.
Now it has surfaced is here for life
Will never let it slip by again
My wonderful God is with me to the end
Will never let him go again
He is forever mine for the rest of my life.

Feeling Peace Within Myself Once Again

Feeling peace within myself once again
I sit here and listen to the sound of peace within me
It feels so good listening to the sound it makes
Where have you been all my life, wonderful peace?
It is so nice to have that lovely warm feeling within;
Waited a lifetime for this feeling to return to me.
I am so happy that I am able to feel it once again
The last time I felt like this was when I was a baby.
No more worry or care in the world was there then
I have missed this feeling I had then so much
I once again receive it with open arms like I did then
I am so glad that we can rejoin once again
Please I ask you never leave me again by myself
I am your friend forever and ever and ever
I am always going to be here and will never let you go
Thank you for coming back to me once again
This time it's for the rest of my life until the end
I will never let you leave me again like you did before
Mine for keeps and no one will ever take you away from me
Lovely peace, thank you for coming back to your rightful owner.

**(Note: I promised the next poem that I did would be a happy
one. Well, this is how I am feeling now. Hope it helps someone,
as life doesn't always stay the same--it can get better.)**

Rahki

My brothers I tied rakhi on
Tied a knot with all my love
Just to say I am your big sister;
You gave me gifts in return.
I accepted with all my heart,
As they were given with love.
Gave you sweets in your mouth;
That was my love to you.
When your sister needed you most in life,
You were nowhere to be seen;
Not a thought or a call.
You loved me once, I thought
What happened to our love we shared?
I know there will be no rakhi this time;
I was only a sister in name.
There was no love on your part--
I am and always will be that sister you deserted;
will still be here with my memories that we shared.
I will tie a rakhi in my mind;
Accept it and imagine I am next to you.
You will be on my mind
As that is all I have left--
Memories of you and me.

**Rakhi Bandhan is a Hindu festival when you tie a thread on
your brother's hand. It is to show each other your bond that
you share.**

My Lovely Eyes are Sparkling Once Again

Looked into the mirror and saw my eyes smiling back at me
They were so full of joy; that contented look happy to return to its
rightful owner,
Bright and sparkling like the sunshine that was glaring so bright
Never have I seen that gleam in my eyes before this time
Had to look into the mirror twice—no, three times-- to believe
Did those eyes really belong to me; am I their owner?
How did I come to get this look once again
I can't recall seen that look within me before
I liked it so much I kept looking at those eyes
Had a giggle out loud; no one was around to share
I love this new me that I have become
I love myself-yes I do.

**Another happy poem from me. Yes, I am happy and it feels so
good. Last night I noticed my eyes were sparkling. Was so
lovely seeing that. Kept looking in the mirror and smiling.**

This is How I am Feeling

This is how I am feeling happy as I could ever be
No more thinking and in thought
Those sad times have sure gone
Far away deep in my thoughts
Only have happy feelings now
No more looking back at that time
For now I am a happy girl
With lots of love to give with smiles
Can be that little girl again
Came out from my inner self
Was hidden deep in within
My hand was held by God
He pulled me out of my shell
You're not to go back there again
The path you was on you took
Walked it well, you did.
You can enjoy your life now
Be a happy and giving soul
That's your gift from me to you
You have done your time
No more looking back--
Only forward.

Go for Walks with No Care in the World

I go for walks with no care in the world
Looking at people doing their daily tasks
Feeling the fresh breeze touching my face
Meeting people who I talk to
I do a lot of positive talking
Telling them I have found God
They ask how did you do that
I pause for a second and think,
"What shall I say now?"
Quickly, I say it doesn't matter how I got here
Took forty years to get here
Have found God and it's my duty to do his work
I am working for God now
He has chosen me
I will do his work with love

Sit There Relaxed Mind Blank

Sit there, relaxed; mind blank,
Feet flat on the floor.
Breathing in positive energy and negative out;
I can relax myself
Finding it so easy now,
Feeling my aura around me;
Those vibes I feel so calming
Then I feel positive energy within.
This is my time; might be ten minutes or more
Have done all my daily chores
Everyone is happy so I can enjoy my time
My time with God
He has waited patiently for me
I am free of my pain
Can relax now and enjoy
This is my relaxing time
My time with God--just me and him.

Be Positive in Everything You Do

As I go around doing my chores
See many happy faces
I ask lots of question
Am surprised at the response
As before, this would never happen
I am positive and it shines
Be positive in everything you do
Do it from the heart with love
It will shine through
Everyone will see the new you
This is your time to be free
Giving out lots of love
Help whoever comes your way
They have being sent by God
You are working for him now
Hold their hand tight
I am here to help you;
Want to put a smile on your face.

Get No Calls from Them Now

Get no calls from them now;
That's ok, as I have my memories.
Memories I will treasure,
Mostly bad; but some were good,
They are buried deep inside.
Have my memories, so I don't need to see you;
I'll meet you when our time is up.
Our family are waiting on the other side,
and we will be all together again
You enjoy your life,
I am sure enjoying mine.
A very happy person I have become--
You have missed seeing the new me.

Had an Experience Late at Night

Late at night, I had an experience
Someone holding me tight
Didn't know who it was
Said in my mind, "If you're not from the light,
Please leave right away,"
Then I saw a beautiful person,
In spirit form she was
Sitting beside me, she was
Before I could ask her a question
I heard a voice saying, "Mummy, Mummy"
Saw a gorgeous little boy
He was my son I lost;
A few years ago that was
the feeling was overwhelming and when they left,
I was left with a lovely feeling--
I'll hold this memory until we meet again.

I was already upstairs in bed, but I felt someone pick me up at the stairs and bring me up into bed. I saw a squiggly animal. This didn't scare me as all night I have been asking my guide to help me with my fear. This thing was hugging me. I asked if it was from the light. It said " no", so I said "could you go away then?"

He went after I asked him twice. This is when my guide stepped in. I have seen her once before. She has black hair. She said "well done" about how I had sent away the strange snake-shape.. I was awake, as I was talking to her with my mouth open. I asked her if she has being with me all my life. Before she could answer, I heard a child calling 'mummy, mummy' excitedly, as if saying he was pleased to see me. I saw this lovely 4-year-old dressed in cream. He looked like my two sons. I picked him up and put him in my bed with me and my guide. I thought it was my baby, but it wasn't, as there was no way he could have come out of his room, since it has a gate on it. Then all of a sudden, they both disappeared. I lay in bed awake, wondering about my baby that I never had. Just glad I met him. I was fully awake when all this happened.

This is My Home Where I Belong

This is my home where I belong
Was lost in my thoughts before
My family are here holding me tight
Can feel the warmth feeling from them
They sure do love me for what I am
Being accepted for the person I become
This is me the way it should be
Got the rest of my happy days
Will spend them with family
That has accepted me for who I am

No more fear

I lived in fear,
but not anymore.
I was scared;
now I am free.
This is the new me;
No more fear,
no more terror;
No more flashbacks--
I am I.
You will like the new me.

Bird flying

I am that bird flying high in the sky;
I am going to climb higher and higher.
Am I halfway to my destination already?
I will be taking all my friends with me.
Together we will fly higher and higher, until God says
"There will be peace in the world".
Only then can we climb back down
To enjoy this wonderful life--
Life that we are blessed with.

Inner Secret

Now I have found my beliefs within.
There is no one I can share with.
If I tell someone, I get shouted at.
This is my secret, all to myself
I will enjoy, with an open mind
My way, my path that I will take
Used to being on my own;
I know I am not though; I have

a big family in spirit form
They will never leave me by myself.
I will live someone else's way, for now,
So at least I can talk about God
In their way, if not mine.
I love God so much it hurts.
Sensed spirit yesterday
No one to share my joy with;
For now it's my secret to keep.
Thanked them for coming back;
Waiting on my instructions.

I'll be patient, as I have been.
I work for God, I am his helper;
Help me keep my secret
By not letting me get too excited.
I'll hold every thought within,
although that's going to be hard,
as I am used to sharing
The wonderful experiences I gain.
I will be fine, as I have others I share with;
Friends that is, not my family.

I really enjoyed writing this poem. As I wrote this poem my Guide
was with me. Nice violet water smell.

Mom on my mind as I work

Smiled all day doing my work,
Making friendly conversations,
Saying how happy I am today;
Making everyone smile with me.
Then I remembered what Mom said,
and felt choked and in pain again.
How can she ask that of me?
Before, it would have been a straight no;
Now, I sit here thinking, "shall I do it for her?"
Have never done anything for her.
Those were her words to me;
I will try to find a way to do this.
If I come off my path that I am following;
Do what she wants of me,
So we can be together when our time is up;
She says there was no love,
If we are together in the end
We can learn to love again.
Oh, those tears are with me too;

I sit here thinking very hard.

"No" is the answer I am hearing;

This is the right path for me.

I will continue with what's deep inside me,

As I know this is the right way.

Phone call from mom

Phone rings; its Mom calling.
Heart skips a beat;
Is it bad news she's sharing?
I pick up the phone
Hello, it's your mom she says
Everything ok I ask nervously
All is well said in a faint voice
Don't like these sorts of calls
She still isn't free of this pain
Feel it in her voice I do
Can you do something for me?
Think for a moment what can she mean
You have never done anything for me
Do this one thing for me
What I ask nervously waiting

Unbelievable what she asked of me
I said I would for her
In the end, I am going to follow my heart
Will give it a go just for you
So she can't say I didn't try
I have my God that I follow
Who is holding my hand very tight?
Will follow yours for you
So you can't say I don't do anything for you
If we both follow the same God
Maybe we can be together when our time is up
That's the words from mom
Together in paradise which is our home
In the end, there is only one God
No matter which way you go
You know what's right and wrong

My life as it is Today

ope you enjoyed reading my poems and didn't get too sad. I know you would have felt the sadness as you read each poem. Don't be sad, as I have matured into a lovely beautiful woman who has with time, and with me sorting my past out, grown and learned how to be the new me. My last few poems are how I am feeling right now and I intend to remain that person, as I like it so much.

I missed out in giving out the love that I always had hidden deep within me. I have found my inner peace and life is much better. At the end of my ordeal, I received the gift of God's hand. God is deep inside me and He is here for the rest of my living days. My role in this life is to do my duties as a wife, mother and friend. At the same time, I am working with God. God found me and it's my duty as His helper to help others. If only by words or meeting, He will send them to me and I will receive them with open arms.

I have seen that light, and am going back to that dark place to reach out to others. I will show them the way. Together, we can go to the light. I was told my life was going to change, but I was not prepared for such a big change and now I can't stop smiling. Believe me; life does get better, as I am finding out.

Never in a million years did I think I would write a book, and then find a publisher. Dreams do come true, as I found out. You have to believe in your dreams, and only then will they come true. My dream has been granted, and I am enjoying the journey. People stop me and ask why I am smiling. I enjoy telling others how I got to my happy stage.

Along your path in life, you will be sent opportunities. Look very closely, as they can be missed. Then you will be sent angels, who will reach for your hand and hold it tight. Listen to your heart, and your inner feelings. This is the true you, who will never lie. I am so happy, it's just unbelievable. I want to spread peace into people's lives and I will. My life is going to get even better, as all my bad times have passed. Now it's my time to help others and at the same time, I won't forget myself as I am very important too.

I want to say to you live a positive life, be happy, and do well in everything you touch. God is watching you, and you will be answerable to Him when your time is up. Inner peace is available to everyone, but in order to get it, you have to deal with what is deep inside you. Once you start to do this, gradually, you will get to your intended destination. There will be obstacles in the way, but you will know what is right. Follow your heart and listen to your feelings. They will lead you to the correct path planned for you.

Be positive in everything you do and do it with love, as this is you. You will be led away from your path, but be strong and keep to the path. It took me forty years to get to where I am now. You will know when the time is right for you to go on your journey. I went searching for answers and that took me 20 years. It was not an easy journey and I asked many questions.

You have to do it for yourself as no- one is going to do it for you. It is your life, your responsibility. I discovered my answers along the way and learned a great deal on my journey on the path I took. The answers at the time did not really make sense, but towards the end of my journey, they have started to make themselves clear to me. Missing pieces of the jigsaw puzzle slowly came together towards the end. I now feel grounded with my feet firm and flat on the floor. With these answers, I know exactly where I am going with my life. For the first time in my life, I have goals and plans that I want to achieve for me.

Yes, you can be easily led away as I found out with just one phone call. It just takes one person to pull you back from your intended path. I did think for a second, as you may have noticed from my last two poems. Then again, you would do anything for your mother, but when the roles are reversed, I found that for me that was not the case. I am therefore sticking to the path that I am on. I believe this is the correct way to continue with my peace within. This is the right way for me and if I do make mistakes along the way, I will find my way back and continue with the journey that was planned for me before I was born.

I am very happy and content with my life that I hold so dear, even though in my fight for justice, I lost all my blood family. It is very sad but in the end, there was no true love on their part. Not one of them stood with me when I was putting my past right. Only my husband and my two sisters- in- law were with me. I found it upsetting as I had protected my family all my life. I stayed silent so they could have a better life but in the end, I could not live with the pain anymore. As I started to put my past right step by step, I was gaining my inner peace. I started to meditate and found I could empty my mind. As I had a clear mind, I could focus and was able to receive vibes, feel my aura, and be at complete peace. I would describe it as magical and so relaxing. I still continue with my meditations and enjoy them very much. I talk to God all day long and thank Him for my life that I hold so dear.

I work with the public, and this has given me opportunities to give out so much unconditional love. The love I give out, I get back twenty-fold. I walk around with a big smile on my face, and share my story with whomever I meet. I just cannot stop smiling, as I am truly happy.

During the last conversation I had with Mom she asked me to leave my religion and follow hers, in order that when we both die we can be together again. I did think about doing this but in the end, I followed my own advice. It took my forty years to get to the place I am at now. I am not going back to that dark place that I came from. I like it where I am at with my life and I intend to

141

continue on the path set out for me.

I know there was no love on her part, as she keeps reminding me. I would have preferred not knowing that she felt that way about me. She didn't understand what happened to me. She followed what everyone else told her. For me, I have lots of love for her and always will. She is my mom and I love her dearly. My dream is that one day my book be converted to Punjabi, so that my mom could read what her daughter went through; something she is not able to understand. I have given up trying to help her do so, as she always puts the blame back on me.

I do still crave my family's love, I admit. I was brought up in a very large family, a family that is well respected. There were many of them, who all said they loved me and foolishly I believed them. They said they thought of me; I believed them, they said they understood me; I believed them.

When my little voice got bigger, theirs became softer; little by little, they have all become a distant memory.

My brothers and cousins--well that's a different story. I adored and felt that I loved all the family--but they meant the world to me, I have always felt that I had a strong bond with them, and I long for their affection. I am beginning to learn that it is always going to be a one- way thing. In time, it will all become a distant thought, just like my past which is now over and done with. I will move on from this craving, as I have already seen it happen, not on my part but on theirs. They erased me from their lives, and that taught me a lesson: to move on and live my life and stop craving for what will never be. My pain will lessen in time, I know. A day will come when they need me, but it will be too late. They chose my abusers over me - something I will never understand.

My next book

While you have been reading this book, I am in the process of writing another. I am happy, but when I think about Mom, it makes me sad. The next book will be about our relationship.

On the other hand, it could be something completely different, as I do not know what spirit have planned for me on my journey ahead. Only time will tell what is in store for me. I sense it to be a good thing and something I will never forget in this lifetime. I believe that I am a generation of souls who have lived many lives on this earth plane and I have fulfilled my last role. God planned this life before I was born into this world, which was chosen for me and God attached free will to my life. With this free will, other people changed my destiny. Be it good or bad, I believe that someone else can change your path. So I know it's not my fault that something bad happened to me. But I fixed it and got back onto the right path that was originally chosen for me. A child can't be blamed for creating those experiences themselves.

We will see what spirit has in store for me. At the moment all I can see is that I am a guide for others--to help them heal.

It is time to say goodbye, tears
Not in this lifetime
Nor the next
Don't want to experience
Life like
This again.
The next life I plan
Will be joyful;
now that will be nice,
Won't it? Yes, it will.

Life does get better, peace within is found again.

Spiritual 'blogs' that I have recorded over the years

There is a difference between spirituality and religion. All I know is that today I finally made myself ready to receive whatever God has for me… and this has been an extremely wonderful experience and a blessing.

Each day I learn more about myself than I have in the past 40 years. I have come to terms to with many things in my life; I felt and saw a massive show of energy and strength rise from within me. It is well worth the journey and I know this is just the beginning. Through meditation, I will continue this path, and embrace the feeling of closeness with God.

My first meditation

I decided to meditate for the first time today. I did it for a few minutes and I found I could focus.

Mom had mentioned to me to think of her priest; I tried to visualise him and nothing came. Instead, I saw another priest: an elderly male with a white beard, wearing a turban. I could see what looked like a shawl wrapped over his shoulders. I couldn't see his face.

When I mentioned it to Mom, she told me the priest I had seen is classed as a high priest in her religion. He only comes to the chosen ones, and Mom said I was very lucky to have seen him.

I did question myself. Did I--have I--really seen him? Mom said I did.

Had a visit from my Guide this morning

I felt a presence whilst I was laying in bed, half-awake, I had a feeling it was my Guide and a woman; a cuddly woman. I asked 'are you from the light?' but there was no answer. I said leave if you are not. I asked again 'are you from the light' the answer 'yes' came with a giggle.

I felt she was giggling as I have come such a long way with my mediumship skills. I asked her to hold my hand and she did. I could not see her face, as I couldn't move my body.

When I met my Guide last year, she said to me 'Love yourself', I had never forgotten those words. I didn't know what she meant at that time, but I do now. I do love myself and am proud of what I have achieved. I wanted to ask her many questions that were going on in my head at the time, but the baby woke up. Last time I had a visit from my Guide, my son in spirit came and wanted his mummy. Maybe next time I will have more time with her.

Had an experience last night

Last night there was spirit in my room. I felt it on my bed. Then I felt the spirits presence around me. I felt hands around my neck. I asked if it was my guide, there was no reply; I asked it to go away. Then I saw a Moses basket on my dresser. I asked if I was going to have a baby. A quick yes came. I am not planning a baby so could this mean something else? To me, it meant a new beginning.

That night my little one was not feeling well he had a raised temperature, as Id settled him he would constantly wake up as he said he had seen a monster. He kept pushing whatever this was off his legs. All night whatever it was with him kept him awake all night. Not knowing and confused about what to do, I constantly asked the presence to go away and told my little one to do the same. This incident happened before I had my experience.

Angels showing me that they are watching over me

One morning as I opened the front door I found two fifty pence pieces. They were lined up together, I think with heads facing upwards. As I got into work and on my cash register there was two 2 pence's. At the end of my shift, someone handed me another two pence's which were on the floor. The next day I found one pence on the floor. Angels are showing me that they are with me and these are pennies from heaven.

Step closer to meeting my guide.

I wasn't going to meditate last night, but thought ten minutes wasn't a long time. So I did. I felt a very strong presence. It was making my heart race. I just panicked and came out of my meditation. I felt the presence was still with me afterwards. I started to panic and went online and asked a medium friend for advice. They reassured me it was my guide getting me used to their presence. I am so glad I have somewhere I can go if I feel I need an answer.

I feel I am getting closer to meeting my guides and I am taking it easy. I hope my experience will help others starting out.

Last night I saw my guide and my baby that I lost 4 years ago

I went to bed around 5 o'clock yesterday and woke up at 11pm. I felt peckish; so made myself some toast. (Ok, I was tired).

I did finally go upstairs to bed; but I felt as though someone had picked me up at the stairs and put me up into bed. I saw a squiggly animal; very bushy; rubbing against my body. I asked if it was from the light. It said, "no," so I said, "can you go away?" It went after I had asked it twice.

I wasn't scared, as all night; I had been asking my guide to help me with my fear. This is when my guide stepped in. I had seen her once before. She said, "Well done," for my asking the strange shape to go away. I was awake, as I was talking to her with my mouth open. I asked her if she has been with me all my life. Before she could answer, I heard a child calling "mummy "excitedly as saying he was pleased to see me. I saw this lovely 4-year-old dressed in cream. He looked like my two sons. I picked him up and put him in my bed with me and my guide. I thought it was my baby but it wasn't, I then realised my children were fast asleep and could not have got out of the room as I had a safety gate there. Then all of a sudden they both went. I was left wondering about my baby that I had lost a few years ago. Just glad I met him, was nice and sad at the same time. I was fully awake when all this happened. I did not doubt myself as I normally do.

Sensing spirits at work

I have being sensing spirits around me a lot at work for a while now. The smell is strong in the ladies' changing rooms. For months, I have been asking my colleagues if they can smell anything. They have all said no. It was strong yesterday. I went for a quick break and the smell had gone on my return. I think it was spirit letting me now as I have been doubting myself.

In my working day my Guide is standing beside me. I can sense a lovely violet smell; it makes me feel nice and it's welcoming. I don't tell anyone and I keep it to myself, as I wouldn't know how to explain my experiences.

Really enjoying my meditations

I have being really enjoying my meditations lately. I can hear music, but it feels as if it is in the distance. I feel someone with me. I don't know who, but they are making me feel so comfortable. I am just taking it very slowly though by doing 5 to 10 minutes a day. I am feeling much more relaxed.

Want to share an out of body experience I had 10 years ago

This was the time I was having lots of OBEs. This one time, I saw two Japanese women. They were wearing shiny blue outfits, and very pretty. They were taking me somewhere. I was floating. Behind me, were people all dressed in black following us? It was so hot. They were just holding me. I don't now where they were taking me. I said I was too hot. The next thing I was back in my cold bedroom. Was amazing experience, one which I will never forget.

Had a visit from a lady spirit this morning

Relaxing and wide awake this morning just lying in bed. A spirit of a woman came to me and said to me, "Love yourself." Then she went in a flash, and everything was so nice. This was the first time I felt that I had seen this spirit during the day. It happened so quickly. All I can remember she had dark hair and tan skin.

Had an experience before waking up

As I was waking up this morning, I felt a heavy presence above my head. Felt calm and relaxing. It was spirit but not sure what or who. I felt as if I was in a trance. The feeling was really relaxing. Felt like another dimension above my head--from another world.

Conversation with my Guide about my past

"I was lying in bed, fully awake and my head on top started to hurt. The pain was so intense, I decided to get up and ground and protect. At this point I had an astral experience. Was magic, didn't go anywhere, just floated in the room. I came back to my body and the pain in my head was still there. I asked who ever was with me are you from the light. I did get something but can't remember what. I asked my primary guide to step in. I asked are you from the light. She giggled and said yes. I have had this guide with me before, so I recognised her voice. She had a conversation with me and said she has being with me all my life. She spoke about the time I got engaged at seventeen. She said she was glad I didn't go through with it. Her voice was so clear and I could hear her.

Thank you spirit world for being with me

I just want to thank the spirit world for being with me all my life. I was panicking today, regarding getting my book together. I needed to submit all my work on Monday to publishers, and still hadn't got a front cover. Then there's the editing, and other little problems.

But, I did a prayer to the spirit world, and said as it was their idea for me to do this book, please help me. What do you know, it's all coming together. My lovely friend is doing my front cover, and editing my book.

The spirit world is always listening to us. So always listen to your thoughts and feelings. It's the spirit world sending one of their signals and telling you to do something.

To change the world first you must change you.

o change the world, first you must change you. I have done that and that's why my book is called "Life does get better Peace within is found again. It is so amazing finding the real you. I am so lucky to have found inner peace in my 40's. Someone can search a lifetime, and still not find their inner peace.

I got here by asking questions and standing up for myself. Life is a challenge and we will always be tested. Find that strength that you hold close to you and be that strong person that you have become. In my journey I did lose all of my blood relatives but I was rewarded with a gift--the Hand of God, as I do feel he is deep within me. I have Guides that stand with me on this wonderful journey. I can't communicate with them yet, but I will one day. That dream is on hold until I get my business up and running. Remember all dreams come true. If you don't believe that start believing and make that dream come alive.

Someone asked me today how they can find their inner peace.

First step look at your life and if something needs sorting, sort it. Second step love yourself first and only then will you be able to show love to others. Always be positive and give out unconditional love to anyone you may meet. Even love your enemy as one day they too will need guidance. You don't have to tell them to their face just send out positive vibes.

As you go through life and finely see the end in sight. It is emotional looking back at what once was and how far you have come. What a journey I have had and look at what is waiting for me at the top of this amazing ladder of life. My message to you all as always is this: if something needs fixing, it's your life, your responsibility and you're in charge of your life. So stand up and take back what was already yours. Take back control. There will still be times when you fall back down, but be strong and stand up and fight. There is a lot of support out there. Strangers who you would never have met will reach out their hand. Hold that hand tight and never let go. Have faith in yourself as you are strong. Be that person that your heart desires and I will be there giving you strength, if not in person then spiritually. I will never let go of your hand--and that's a promise.

Life Does Get Better

Peace within is found again

Sara Khan

Useful contact details

I would like to thank the following people who helped me produce this book:

Photography by: R Ahmed www.studio68.org.uk who designed my book cover.

Mona Adam

Aman TV Production House

Gary Peacock, Midland Hotel, Forster Square, Bradford BD1 4HU

Fatima Patel, Managing Editor for Asian Sunday Newspaper

Xpressions Hairdressers, Shipley Bradford
http://www.mediumystic.com/forums/welcome.php
https://www.facebook.com/Sarahcaan.co.uk

Riff Haworth

RH Media Inc for their continued support

Gary Hill: Photography

https://twitter.com/GDHphotography

http://gdhphotography.blogspot.org

http://www.napac.org.uk/survivors
Free phone 0800 085 3330
http://www.rapecrisis.org.uk/

Free Phone National Helpline: 0808 802 9999 158 12-2.30pm/7-
http://www.ibiblio.org/rcip/partners.html

https://sarakhanblog.wordpress.com/

Hope they help anyone else who is going through a difficult time. There is a lot of help out there so do not be afraid to ask. These websites helped me.

What I am doing at present: Sara Khan: Today 2016

had an overwhelming feeling to pray for people, so I decided to set up a website where individuals can leave names. With the help of my Guides, I pray for others. I am writing a book, and the title is "He said yes" My husband has said I can attend a circle to develop as a medium. That was my initial aim until I had a sudden urge, a feel from within, this again directed me in another direction in life.

16196917R00101

Printed in Poland
by Amazon Fulfillment
Poland Sp. z o.o., Wrocław